'Autism in the words of autistic people. Alongside fascinating individual tales of personal triumphs, this collection of insights and tales shows the amazing reflection, articulation and self-awareness of these autistic authors. This book is surely a must for parents of autistic children to let them see into the future and inspire them to know what their children have the capacity to become.'

– Sarah Hendrickx, autistic adult, Autism Specialist and author

Bittersweet on the Autism Spectrum

Books in the same series

Love, Partnership, or Singleton on the Autism Spectrum
Insider Intelligence
Edited by Luke Beardon and Dean Worton
ISBN 978 1 78592 206 0
eISBN 978 1 78450 484 7

Aspies on Mental Health: Speaking for Ourselves
Insider Intelligence
Edited by Luke Beardon and Dean Worton
ISBN 978 1 84905 152 1
eISBN 978 0 85700 287 7

Asperger Syndrome and Social Relationships
Adults Speak Out about Asperger Syndrome
Edited by Genevieve Edmonds and Luke Beardon
ISBN 978 1 84310 647 0
eISBN 978 1 84642 777 0

Bittersweet on the Autism Spectrum

Edited by Luke Beardon, PhD
and Dean Worton

Jessica Kingsley *Publishers*
London and Philadelphia

First published in 2017
by Jessica Kingsley Publishers
73 Collier Street
London N1 9BE, UK
and
400 Market Street, Suite 400
Philadelphia, PA 19106, USA

www.jkp.com

Library of Congress Cataloging in Publication Data
Names: Beardon, Luke, editor. | Worton, Dean, editor.
Title: Bittersweet on the autism spectrum /
edited by Luke Beardon and Dean
Worton.
Description: London ; Philadelphia : Jessica Kingsley Publishers, 2017.
Identifiers: LCCN 2016032926 | ISBN 9781785922077
Subjects: LCSH: Asperger's syndrome--Patients--Personal narratives. |
Autistic people--Rehabilitation.
Classification: LCC RC553.A88 B525 2017 | DDC 616.85/88200922-
-dc23 LC record available at https://lccn.loc.gov/2016032926

British Library Cataloguing in Publication Data
A CIP catalogue record for this book is available from the British Library

ISBN 978 1 78592 207 7
eISBN 978 1 78450 485 4

Printed and bound in Great Britain

MIX
Paper from
responsible sources
FSC® C013056

*To all those autistic individuals who have inspired
me and taught me so much; and my family –
as always, without you, I am nothing.*
Luke Beardon

*I would like to dedicate this book to all my family and
friends, and all those who have been there for me in
my life, and to Genevieve Edmonds who inspired these
books to be written, and will never be forgotten.*
Dean Worton

CONTENTS

PREFACE

Luke Beardon

It is with the greatest of pleasure that I am able to introduce a book on positive experiences as articulated by adults on the autism spectrum. Autism means so many different things to so many different people – rightly so, as of course all autistic people are individuals in their own right, with their own unique sets of experiences and ways of understanding the world around them. Having noted that, it is not at all uncommon to find autism within outlets such as the media being used alongside rather pejorative terms, which, however subtly, can create a sense of negativity associated with autism. Whilst it is absolutely the case that some people are impacted negatively for whatever the reason, it is equally clear that this is not a global experience and, for some, being autistic is not all doom and gloom. One of my ex-doctoral students, for example, becomes incensed when she is described as 'suffering with autism'; as she so brilliantly states, 'I am blessed to be different. Without autism the world might be quite dreary.'[1]

When I have written about the positive side of autism publicly in the past, the feedback has been very clearly divided: the majority of people (almost exclusively people with autism) are grateful that a positive side of being autistic is being explored, but a minority has noted that in their experience there is nothing positive about autism at all. I am fully aware that autism is expressed in a plethora of ways, and presentations can be wildly different. In this book Dean and I have very deliberately chosen to provide

---

1   Beale-Ellis, S. (2015) *Autism and Martial Arts: A Guide for Children, Parents and Teachers*. Herne Bay: NAKMAS Publishing, p.4.

a platform upon which individuals themselves can express what positive experiences they have had as an autistic person. There are many other books that directly target problems associated with autism; this one, rightly or wrongly, has chosen a different path, one that we feel is not just valid but also illuminating.

We didn't really know what to expect when we embarked on this book. Probably a good thing – in many ways autism is a rather unpredictable field! However, we were extremely pleased when we started to get sample chapters sent in and realised the richness and diversity of experiences that people were writing about. I won't pick and choose chapters for individual praise – they are all a very worthy read. What is so illuminating to me is that some of the subject areas that individuals have related as positive could never have been predicted in the proverbial 'million years'.

Without a clear evidence base it's impossible to know what the general perspective on autism is within society; however, I would be willing to bet that 'autism' and 'positive experiences' are not usually paired up together at the forefront of people's minds. Just because one is autistic it does not automatically mean that positive experiences are preclusive. This book demonstrates that individuals can, and do, experience life in positive ways, sometimes in the face of adversity.

I do not subscribe to the notion that one must have a problem before one is identified as being autistic. To me, this makes little (or no) sense. Being autistic does not necessarily mean that one has a problem. Very often, being autistic means that life may be harder in many ways – but lots of people face all sorts of problems, autistic or otherwise. 'Diagnostic criteria' tend to suggest that people with autism are somehow 'lacking' – i.e. that they are impaired in some way. This very medical 'deficit based' model can be hugely offensive to some autistic people. There are some who would sooner suggest that the only 'deficit' is in lacking a similar cognitive profile to the predominant neurotype – and, further, who might suggest that this is in itself not a deficit at all. Being a minority group will often mean that there are challenges to face that are less common within the majority population; it does not automatically mean that being in that minority group means that one is inferior in some way.

In a sense, this book is about celebrating the positive experiences of people with autism. It is not trying to suggest that all autistic people will share positive experiences, or even to infer that there are any particular themes or trends in what people with autism experience as positive. Just reading through the chapters gives a very clear message that what is positive to one person may not fall into that category for another. However, reading the chapters does give a very strong message that some autistic individuals can experience life in a positive way, and there are elements of passion, humour and intensity of emotion that make this book such a rewarding read.

I would like to thank the authors for putting their time and energy into submitting their chapters, and Dean for all his invaluable input.

Chapter 1

Opening the Umbrella
(Multicoloured Thank You Very Much!)

Alyssa Aleksanian

Introduction by Luke Beardon

The following is such a powerful quotation it seems appropriate to start with it:

> *The privilege of being oneself is a gift many take for granted, but for someone with AS, being allowed to be oneself is the greatest and rarest gift of all.*

Alyssa is a gifted writer and the quotation above illustrates how superb she is at articulating her thoughts. The chapter as a whole is stimulating and insightful.

I think that one of the key messages, so brilliantly delivered in the chapter, is that so much can be gained by first allowing an individual to identify with themselves; second, for those around them to understand the individual and accept them for who they truly are – as opposed to who they may historically have tried to be. So many adults that I have the privilege of speaking to tell me of the relief of getting an identification and subsequently feeling empowered to stop emulating others, or trying to be what others want them to be (i.e. more in line with the general population). I don't think it's a case of 'just letting people with autism/Asperger's syndrome (AS) behave in any way they want', which is a criticism I have heard in the past, and nor do I think that this is a sentiment that people with autism/AS see as appropriate either; however, what is clear to me is that allowing an individual to understand themselves and develop the confidence to engage with the world and be accepted as a person with autism/AS is critical. Perhaps, one day, this will be more common than 'the rarest gift of all'.

Diagnosis as an adult

Early in life I recognised the different tune humming through me, out of synch with other children my own age. Not with nature, not with the rhythms of the planet; those songs I understood. But with the world – the 'peopled world' – those harmonies were a constant clash.

It has often been said that many people with AS identify with the unpeopled world, whether it be nature, machines or the arts. Take the unpredictability of 'humanity' out of our life's equation and our AS anxiety drops to a mere murmur.

For years, all those quirks (which on a bad day I called my 'random defects' and on a good day I called 'just being me') I kept tightly under wraps. I had learnt early on that to say certain things got me stared at, stony silence or edged out of a conversation. I thought that when I reached that magical and elusive age called 'adulthood', all would fall into place and I'd finally hit my stride, somehow catch up to everyone else and work out what they were all on about. I would gesture, laugh and participate with ease – just like I saw others do. However, no elusive age arrived and the eventual catalyst for appreciating my own rhythm came in a very different guise: a diagnosis of Asperger's, well into my thirties.

My diagnosis seemed to happen by chance, but if truth be told, I'm a big believer that nothing happens by chance.

As a school teacher, I come across a lot of children. One given year I had a child arrive in my class who had been diagnosed with Asperger's syndrome. Wanting to be prepared and give this child the best opportunity to learn, I decided to do some research. In my quest for information, I remember picking up Rudy Simone's book *Aspergirls* (2010, Jessica Kingsley Publishers) at a bookstore. I casually flicked through a few pages; paused here and there; read just enough to raise an eyebrow. I shut it a little too quickly, put it down and walked away. A few moments later I was drawn back to the book. I flicked through a few more pages, swallowed hard, put it down and again walked away. When I was pulled back to that bookshelf for a third time, as I picked up the title and stared at the cover, I heard a distinct voice inside my head say 'buy this book'.

I did.

I read that book and as I did, I realised I was reading about myself. And I cannot tell you the relief that washed over me.

I know such an idea sounds strange – suddenly discovering one has a recognised medical dysfunction[1] *and* feeling relief, but allow me to elaborate.

For too many years I had questioned and agonised over why life felt so baffling and people so impenetrable. The cards that life deals – work, relationships, health, tragedies, happiness – all seemed to me like thorny, oversized pills to swallow. Yet, how did other people seem to sail smoothly through these aspects of life? While I felt utterly ill-equipped, many seemed to thrive. Was I was missing a vital tool or piece of information that everyone else had?

---

1   Editors' note: 'medical dysfunction' is a medical model-based way of describing autism; while we recognise that current clinical practice identifies autism in this way, we prefer a social model of autism.

And here I was in a bookstore, reading in a stranger's book all my thoughts, reactions and emotions – a carbon copy of my inner life – secrets that I had never told a soul. Within those pages I found a profound relief that someone, somewhere actually, *finally*, understood.

After some initial research and a recommendation, I made an appointment with a doctor of clinical psychology.

Why the big beautiful umbrella?

Being in that psychologist's office – the waiting, the interview, the assessment – although I was at first acutely nervous, turned out to be a fairly painless process.

For the first time in many, many years, I felt I could actually be myself. As I relaxed back into the couch, the tense mask I had worn each and every day began to slip away. For once, I didn't have to remind myself to look the psychologist in the eyes. I could take my time to speak. It didn't matter if I stumbled over my words or didn't understand her question: I could ask her to repeat it; ask her to be clearer.

The privilege of being oneself is a gift many take for granted, but for someone with AS, being *allowed* to be oneself is the greatest and rarest gift of all.

As she explained my newly acquired, tailored-for-me diagnosis of Asperger's syndrome, the psychologist drew a sweeping arc on her whiteboard. This, she explained, was to represent the autism spectrum under which there were many manifestations, Asperger's being just one. And under autistic spectrum disorder (ASD)[2] there could be over 150 different manifestations, each combination of traits as unique as the individual.

---

2   Autistic spectrum disorder (ASD) is the current clinical term used, for example, in the *Diagnostic and Statistical Manual of Mental Disorders, 5th edition (DSM-5)*; however, it does insinuate that people with autism are all disordered, which is not a concept that the editors subscribe to.

As I listened, staring at the whiteboard, sitting in that office, I remember a clear, striking thought: *that's my umbrella.*

At that very moment a long-held pressure valve deep at the core of me just gave way. *Relief* – I suddenly had an answer, a name for it: *Asperger's.*

Finally, someone else sees me.

The Aspie invisibility cloak

Officially, I come under the banner of 'the invisible Aspie'. I wasn't diagnosed until well into my thirties. I knew nothing about Asperger's; I hadn't heard of the word before I became a teacher – even then I had just a vague understanding. I had been to psychologists before when I was younger. The subject of Asperger's was never raised.

So how did a diagnosis of AS, with all of its blindingly obvious traits, pass me by for almost 40 years? There are many possible reasons.

Diagnosis of AS 25 years ago was in its infancy. Looking back in the literature, diagnosis of boys was prevalent; diagnosis of girls was extremely rare. It is only recent news that girls with AS can manifest very different traits to their male counterparts. As a result, mistakes were made and many children were overlooked. A fair few adults today, aged 40 plus, are just now being diagnosed with AS. For these people, a diagnosis in middle age may mean great upheaval but also that life suddenly begins to make sense.

Growing up I learned to watch others. Girls with AS are more capable of observing social norms than boys, and they are more likely to imitate these norms even though they can't decode or truly understand them. Any girl navigating her way through the teenage years does everything possible to fit in. Girls with AS can do this to an extreme and become excellent mimics, imitators and actors.

Taking into account these factors, it's easy to understand why my Asperger's was invisible.

With any unmasking in life there comes *a seismic shift of the psyche; in other words a remarkable shift of perspective* – both for the one diagnosed and their loved ones. From my personal experience, although dramatic and initially confronting, the diagnosis of AS was an illuminating experience.

What if everyone – parents, teachers, health professionals – all started seeing the diagnosis of AS as a gift? Not autism spectrum disorder, but *autism spectrum difference*?

After all, a diagnosis gives one permission to be one's truest self; why spend years being something that you are not? Finally finding your stride, your true rhythm, can be the key to unlocking great creativity and purpose.

And with such direction, such freedom of expression, one can not only survive but thrive.

After diagnosis: the grief of lost years

Initially after seeking and getting a diagnosis of Asperger's there is relief; the euphoria that a puzzle has been solved. The confused past can be reassessed and future disasters possibly averted.

But then comes the grief. A sadness for lost time; a hindsight that spans over years of confusion, along with the memories and exhaustion of constantly keeping one's head just above water. How much better could life have been if we'd only known?

There is anger too. Anger at others for their lack of understanding; for measuring us by an invisible standard we couldn't hope to meet. Anger at ourselves for tolerating what should never have been tolerated; for bending ourselves into unrecognisable shapes to fit someone else's idea of normal.

There is a period of withdrawal in order to analyse the foggy past and attempts to figure out a way, with our new understanding, into the future. There is the picking over every past relationship and the sifting through of relationships that are now.

Then there are promises made to ourselves, and conversations needed to be broached with others, the revelation of our diagnosis, should they wish to come close to us now.

As with all types of grief, this process takes time. We have lost an old, confused but familiar life and found ourselves in a different future. Some patterns are hard to break; some reactions are difficult to gain an awareness of. But we have a road map now; we are survivors. With a lot of compassion for ourselves and support from others (if we are lucky enough to have it) we will find our way.

I have a theory and a hope

The Theory: Life has taught those of us with AS that the predominant neurotype (PNT) world's responses cannot be predicted or relied upon. We respond as best we can, with what resources we have at any given time, knowing that our tools are perhaps made for a different purpose, a different world.

We do cope; we do survive. We adapt and bridge vast gaps far more than PNTs have to. We are stronger than we think. We wouldn't be here if we weren't. We have survived.

With such a hyper-extension required of our sensitive selves, with other gifts of wonder we discover throughout our lives along the way, a byproduct we unfortunately continue to create is anxiety.

Our platform stands as worry and fear. It becomes an accepted norm; a tolerance; a hum that accompanies us, always throughout our life.

The Hope: We need to change this hum, transmute it, lighten it and instead begin to operate from a platform of awe and wonder. To do so we need to express our childlike exuberance. This I believe is the essential point: joy is our Aspie nature, our birthright, and it comes only through genuine self-expression. This base of worry and fear has been overlaid, layer on top of layer, as our reaction to a society that we perceived did not accept us. We can change this base by living a *life fully expressed on our own terms.*

To be aware of our nature in all its glorious fullness, along with the wonderful authentic and creative way we see the world so that we may finally be ourselves, is a noble life-long aspiration.

Really begin. Start today. Start to see Asperger's as a gift. Turn to your Aspie nature and with all the warmth and compassion within you, say:

Welcome.

And watch life really begin to change.

Chapter 2

How Volunteering with Bradford Autism Support Gave Me Confidence and Helped Me Come to Terms with My Own Diagnosis of Asperger's Syndrome

Gwen Greenwood

Introduction by Luke Beardon

This is a great read – inspirational, really. Gwen's journey to discovery via her voluntary work is an insightful and uplifting one, despite the lows she has obviously been through; in fact, Gwen demonstrates the tenacity and will seen in so many people on the spectrum to fight against difficult times and give back to the world. I think Gwen's message about learning so much from direct contact with individuals is a very important one. Research and books are extremely important, of course. But I do think at times within the autism field not enough credence is given to the invaluable contribution to knowledge that autistic individuals can make; both through spending time with individuals on the spectrum, and listening to people like Gwen who can provide training. One other notable point about this chapter (and there are several I could have mentioned) is that Gwen brilliantly dispels some of the concepts that are sometimes associated with autism. She so clearly has a depth of empathy with those she supports, and her writings on the way in which she and they engage are a very telling point indeed. The notion that 'autistic people lack empathy' certainly needs reviewing!

—

Please note that, while I give my own name, the names of the other people in this story have been altered for their privacy and protection.

—

I've been involved in voluntary work since my early teens. I'm not a religious, or a particularly altruistic person, but my mum firmly believes that volunteering is good for me. Since (like many Aspies) I struggled to maintain an active social life or a paid job while I was at secondary school, it was hard for me to wriggle out of any opportunities to volunteer. Under my mum's guidance I've volunteered at cafés, community centres, village fetes and children's play schemes. I vividly remember one afternoon when I returned from the Tree House Café, my hands chapped and my feet and back aching from several hours of unpaid washing up. I marched up to my mum and told her that was it, I wasn't going to volunteer any more ever again. It's not like I'd even *been* volunteering, since she'd pushed me into all those jobs.

My mum accepted this decision. However, the habit was so engrained that I signed up for a weekly three-hour slot volunteering with Cancer Research as soon as I enrolled at uni. This was probably my least favourite volunteer job. Both the women I worked with were well past the retiring age. Sitting in that shop, smelling the moth balls embedded in clothing and listening to two old ladies bicker and complain about the rest of the world was incredibly tedious, and I felt shocked by how judgemental they could be about people they barely knew. My favourite volunteer job was at the Bluecote art gallery in Liverpool. There were other young people volunteering there, including a gorgeous twenty-something woman with dreadlocks, whom I still wish I'd plucked up the courage to ask out. My role was mostly to keep track of how many people visited the galleries. We were allowed to take a book in with us, and on my first day I got through all of Margaret Atwood's *Negotiating with the Dead*, plus a book of poems by Brecht. I also collected tickets during live events, meaning I often got to see the show for free.

My most rewarding experience with volunteering wasn't at the Bluecote, the Tree House Café or Cancer Research. It was volunteering with Bradford Autism Support (BAS). I did my first summer play scheme there when I was 18, volunteering for two days a week for six weeks. Of course, it was my mum who coerced me into it. But I am so, so glad she did.

On the day of my interview at BAS Mum drove me down in the car. I had swapped my usual black combat boots, corset and thick black eyeliner for a white top, black skirt and natural makeup in an attempt to look more 'professional'. Imagine how foolish I felt when I walked into the office and met my boss – a man wearing ripped jeans, a Cure t-shirt and with messy, Robert Smith-style hair. There's a lesson in that for everyone – always be yourself, because you never know when you might bump into someone who'd love the real you.

The interview went by without any hiccups. I was given a brief overview of my responsibilities, in my boss's words, to get 'down and dirty with the kids', and filled in all the appropriate forms. I decided to work with the younger group on a Monday and Tuesday, which was a mixture of children with Asperger's syndrome, mild autism[1] and classical autism. I've always loved little kids. They're so full of energy, have vivid imaginations and rarely judge me in the same way adults do. When I was asked why I wanted to work with autistic children, what I blurted out shocked everyone, including me: 'Because I have it. I have autism.'

There was a brief moment of silence before the conversation carried on as normal. In truth I was probably more shocked than they were. I'd been diagnosed with Asperger's syndrome and dyspraxia at the age of six and, while that knowledge was always at the back of my mind, I just hadn't come to terms with it. I rarely revealed my diagnosis, and if anyone, even my parents, brought up the fact that I was on the autism spectrum I would abruptly deny it.

My inability to admit that I had Asperger's only made things worse for me, because I couldn't possibly receive support for a disability I wouldn't own up to. During my teenage years I remember feeling very isolated and unable to interact with others. I would either say nothing, or talk for hours about a random special interest, barely pausing for breath or giving the person I was talking to a chance to reply. I described this sense of isolation and separateness as being trapped in a glass box, which I would eventually write the following poem about...

---

1   Mild autism is often used to describe individuals who are intellectually high-functioning; however, it does not mean that the impact of autism on the individual is mild.

The Glass Box

These glass walls,
Thinner than a single layer of skin
Have made me utterly unreachable.
I cannot hear you,
Smell you,
Taste you,
Touch you.
You breathe clean air.
I breathe the same stale air
Of infancy,
Have grown
crooked
And twisted
out of shape
To fit the confines of this space.
The glass thickens.
Shadows start to bleed.
You blur,
distort,
and
We are strangers to each other.

I'm not sure why it was so difficult for me to come to terms with my autism. Perhaps it was because I didn't know any adults who were open about having autism, so I had no role models when growing up. Perhaps it was because I was already bullied for having poor social skills and dressing like a 'Goth'. Perhaps it was because my school had made me feel incredibly guilty for having extra support needs, and some people still think of me as a 'filthy sponger' because I receive Disability Living Allowance (DLA).

Despite having lived with it my whole life, I knew nothing about autism. The first thing I learned working at BAS is that autism is a spectrum disorder. Previously I had assumed everyone with a diagnosis of autism was a bit like me; strange, aloof, but with good verbal skills and able to 'pass' for normal if necessary. I got a big shock on my first day when I walked up to a child, plastered a big grin on my face and said, 'Hello! What's your name?' He ignored me completely. It wasn't that he'd seen me and been overcome by a fit of shyness, or chosen to ignore me because he was rude. He just carried on walking without a moment's hesitation, a blissful, dreamy expression on his face as though he had neither seen nor heard me. I would later find out that this child had Kanner's autism and was completely non-verbal. It would take far more than a simple 'hello' for me to break into his world, and the end result would be far more rewarding.

The six weeks of that play scheme passed by in a blur. Back then I was still in my glass box, rarely talking to the adults who worked there and finding it difficult to initiate conversation with some of the children. I was better at the rough, sensory play that children who craved hard touch needed, such as chasing and wrestling. I sometimes left work with a few bruises and teeth marks, but I didn't mind, as during that time I myself was under-sensitive to pain. I think what I found the most difficult about that first play scheme was the lack of structure. Occasionally we took the kids out to a garden centre, park or swimming pool, but we would often spend six- or seven-hour days at the centre, which had a ball pool, soft play area, bouncy castle and sensory room to keep kids occupied.

Since I had finished my first year of uni a month or two before starting at BAS, it was very rare that I'd get up before 12 or one in the afternoon. The mornings of those play schemes were awful. My body was appalled to be up so early, and often didn't come around until at least two in the afternoon, when I'd already been with the kids for several hours. I think the early mornings were probably just as responsible for my remaining uncommunicative as my Asperger's syndrome. As a volunteer I was eligible for free meals and bus tickets. However, I didn't accept either. Asking for money felt like taking money away from the kids, and I was still such a picky eater that I daren't go to work without my packed lunch.

By the end of the play scheme I started to feel the walls of my glass box getting thinner. I was speaking to staff more and had started noticing what was going on around me. I had also fallen in love with the children I worked with. I would spend hours telling uninteresting, sentimental stories about the kids I worked with to anyone who'd listen. Tom had started talking in more than one word sentences. James gave me a hug last time I played with him on the bouncy castle. Sarah keeps pretending to be my mum and grounding me... I just couldn't help myself. They were small and cute and I was a teenage girl with mothering hormones beginning to course through my body. I loved them all.

Whilst some of the kids I worked with used few words and seemed to rock and flap continuously, others had completely normal behaviour.[2] The children with a diagnosis of high-functioning autism or Asperger's syndrome had good verbal skills, played with each other instead of gravitating towards staff and volunteers, and rarely exhibited challenging behaviour. The only indication they might be different to their neurotypical peers was they were a little too confident and trusting around strangers (an issue that would later come up in my safeguarding training). Countless times, I was greeted with a big hug from a child I had never met before, despite the stereotype that all autistic people hate hugs. If someone who seemed that ordinary could be autistic, then perhaps autism wasn't such a big deal. Perhaps, I might have Asperger's syndrome after all...

Soon, the play scheme was over and I moved to a large, newly built house in Ormskirk, where I would spend my

---

2   Editors' note: we accept that the behaviour of all individuals can be deemed 'normal' to them and that the concept of normality is a subjective one.

second year of uni. I shared that house with three girls whom I was already friends with (one of whom I'd been hopelessly infatuated with ever since I looked into her beautiful brown eyes during freshers' week). A piece of advice for young adults on the autism spectrum: *never* share a house with your friends.[3] Living in close quarters just puts too much pressure on friendships, especially if you have impaired social skills or need a lot of time on your own.

While I did well academically, just about every other aspect of my second year of uni was incredibly difficult. I still hadn't come to terms with my autism, which meant I wasn't acknowledging or getting the right help for the needs I had relating to my disability. I had also put far too much pressure on myself to get the best possible grades. I started self-harming regularly. One day, after hearing my friend make a perfectly innocent comment about how I'd been annoying her, I emptied two bottles of paracetamol and tried to convince myself to overdose. Although I didn't take the pills, I was so distressed that I had to go into hospital anyway, and my parents immediately drove up from Bradford to make sure I was okay. I went home with them, where I spent the next few months attending therapy, getting off my head on prescription drugs and completing the rest of my assignments from home.

By the time the next summer play scheme rolled around I was lonely, bored and desperate to get out of the house. I went to BAS, explained a little about my health situation and signed up to do the full four days a week. I was warned that this would be a big commitment for a healthy person, let alone someone who'd lost weight rapidly and was still heavily medicated for panic attacks. But I'd had enough of being an invalid. I wanted to do something meaningful.

I threw myself into my work, deciding I would make far more effort than before to bond with the staff as well as the

---

3   Editors' note: this is the author's opinion and not one we would
     apply to everyone.

kids. Getting up early enough to go to work was still hell, especially when I had taken quetiapine (an anti-psychotic used to treat my anxiety) the night before. I was told to take this medication in anticipation of stressful situations, for example, a tough day at work. Thank God I never followed that advice! To this day, I still drool uncontrollably 20 minutes after taking the drug. Forty minutes after taking it I fall into a deep sleep, regardless of where I am or what I'm doing. I often remain drowsy the day after taking quetiapine, which makes it harder to care for a roomful of hyperactive autistic kids.

Since I was doing four days a week, I got to spend time with teenagers with Asperger's syndrome and autism, as well as the high support non-verbal group and the autistic children I knew from the Monday/Tuesday sessions. The teenage group has always been the most difficult, but that doesn't have anything to do with their autism. Like most neurotypical teenagers, they're at that age where they're constantly challenging grown ups and feel too embarrassed to take part in 'kids" activities like drama or arts and crafts. I've asked the teenagers I work with what activities they'd like to do over and over, but all they can come up with is watching TV.

On my first day back I wandered around in a quetiapine haze until I saw Tom (a child from last year's play scheme). Suddenly I felt wide awake and I rushed towards him, thinking he'd give me a hug or ask to be picked up and spun round and round like he did the year before. But a year is a long time to any child, especially one with autism. Tom looked right through me, and I realised I was going to have to work hard to re-enter his world again. All the old children seemed to have forgotten me, and there were so many new ones that it felt almost like starting from scratch. However, this time I knew a little more about autism and was familiar with most of the staff.

There were more structured activities and day trips than last year, which made the six-hour working days go by much faster. I was very grateful for these trips, because as a volunteer I had all my expenses paid, and we often took the kids to places I'd never have thought of going by myself, such as Crazy Golf or Tropical World. To be honest, I think the volunteers and staff probably enjoyed these trips more than the kids did.

During those six weeks I got to know some wonderful children, who've taught me more about autism than a textbook ever could. I found the easiest way to engage with the shy ones was to spark up a conversation about their special interest. One child, Raj, was obsessed with horror movies. I don't think he'd actually watched them himself, but he had older cousins who told him about all the films they'd seen. Plus he seemed to have looked up the plot of every horror film in existence on the internet. While we were on the bus together he spotted the *Saw* (a popular horror franchise) key ring I had, and became fascinated with it. I was forced to invent a life, a home, likes and dislikes for 'Baby Jigsaw' off the top of my head. This toy became the gateway to communicating with Raj. When he had something important to say, he would start with 'You know Saw? He wants to tell you something...' before speaking in a low-pitched growl (the voice of Baby Jigsaw).

I did wonder if the staff thought I was a bad influence on this child. I was back in my 'Gothic' clothing, which Raj referred to as 'horror clothes'. While my knowledge of horror films helped me bond with Raj, his constant questions about murderers and exclamations of 'Saw's gonna put you in the death trap!' were probably seen as inappropriate behaviour for a seven-year-old. I later discovered that Raj had been attending the play scheme for months, and never said a word. The staff were probably just glad I'd got him talking.

There were plenty of children at the play scheme who were completely non-verbal. Engaging with them was a much more challenging process, which I did by using brightly coloured, unusually shaped toys and other things to stimulate the senses (e.g. different textured materials to touch, or a fan to create air currents). This sensory play created a lot of mess and was highly unconventional, but the children loved it, and that's all that mattered.

During the summer of this play scheme a wonderful thing happened. The glass walls that had surrounded me since childhood vanished completely. In some ways this left me more vulnerable and exposed than ever. For a while I was prone to fainting and panic attacks, which confused and upset the children I was working with. Professionals say autistic people have limited or no capacity for empathy, but I know that to be untrue. Every time I was ill at work the children were very empathic, giving me hugs, stroking my face and telling me in a very stern voice that I needed to go home and rest. They were far more tolerant and understanding of my illness than most of the neurotypical adults I've come into contact with.

I saw so many of my own struggles in the children I worked with. But I also saw that they were happy, social, confident and productive. There was no reason why I couldn't be all of those things myself. I just needed to adopt a more autism-friendly approach to life. For the first time, I started to talk openly about my Asperger's with friends and family. All thanks to the wonderful children (and staff) who attended BAS! When I looked at my childhood from the point of view of autism, my strange, erratic behaviour suddenly made sense and I felt less isolated. I wasn't a weirdo, a monster or a freak. I was just a little different, and 1 per cent of the world's population were different with me.

I left that play scheme absolutely fascinated with autism. By the time the next summer play scheme rolled around I had put on weight, my mental health had improved significantly and I had a first-class degree in creative writing and drama. Two of the 4500-word papers I produced during my final year of uni were on drama therapy and autism (I started acting at a young age, which really helped me develop social skills and empathy). What I learnt while doing the research for these papers was incredibly valuable, as it helped me to understand myself, and the children I volunteered with.

Like the year before, I volunteered to do every shift on the 2014 summer play scheme at BAS. This time some of the children remembered me, and my new knowledge of autism made it easier to befriend those who didn't. Raj (the child who was obsessed with horror movies), was a little older and a little wiser. When I saw him again, one of the first things he said was 'I know Saw doesn't *really* talk!' in such a knowledgeable, defiant tone that I couldn't help giggling.

There were a great many new children and, although I shouldn't have had favourites, I did. Paul and Amy (who came every Monday) were particularly adorable. Of course, there were the usual trips to swimming pools, crazy golf, the cinema and steam trains, but we also had lots of unstructured time at the centre. I soon got swept into Paul and Amy's elaborate fantasy world, where we played flying pirates, mums and dads, super heroes and a good deal more. Many specialists claim autistic people have limited imaginations – another stereotype these children proved to be untrue! I still remember one funny, imaginative boy who told a hilarious story about turning me into a piece of poo and flushing me down the toilet, only to rescue me from the sewers and transform me back into a human after becoming overwhelmed with guilt.

This time, when the play scheme ended I did not have to move back to Ormskirk as I'd finished uni. I knew it would be hard to find paid work in the current climate, and I was dreading the thought of sitting in my parents' house, filling out endless, mindnumbing job applications. I signed up to volunteer at the youth club sessions BAS holds during term time.

It's been several months, and I am now officially a paid staff member at BAS, meaning I can continue doing what I love. Since the last summer play scheme I have led several drama workshops for autistic children and teenagers, and spoken at autism training sessions for the social services and NHS. I believe that every training programme for autism specialists should include a lecture from someone who's on the autism spectrum, as we know things about autism spectrum disorder (ASD) that aren't in the textbooks, and can explain why children and adults with autism behave the way they do.

Things are still far from perfect. The stress of my job often causes me to overindulge in junk food and drink far more wine than my doctor recommends (I believe people with autism are particularly vulnerable to addiction because we have a pathological need for repetition and routine; if drugs or alcohol become part of that routine, then things can get messy very quickly). I am working to resolve these issues, and on the whole my mental health is the best it's been for years.

Of course, I still make mistakes, and my Asperger's syndrome means I'm not always aware of the appropriate boundaries between myself and the kids. After hugging any child that wanted physical contact for several years, I was recently told that we're not supposed to touch the children at all. I wish this had been stated earlier, but I joined BAS at a time when they were understaffed, meaning I didn't get much training and they were quite relaxed about the rules. It's proving a challenge to stop the kids from hugging me, but I'd like to think I'm rising to the challenge. The reason behind this policy is that autistic children (and adults) often struggle to determine what role a person has in their life. If they can hug the staff at youth club, there's no reason why they can't hug strangers on the street. The non-judgemental, trusting nature of autistic people should be a wonderful thing, but unfortunately it makes us very vulnerable to predators.

Volunteering and working with BAS has undoubtedly been a positive experience for me. It's helped me to come to terms with my own autism, given me lots of opportunities to socialise and I've built a career around it. Despite (and because of) my issues I am very proud to have Asperger's syndrome. And I am very, very proud of the work I do with others on the spectrum.

Chapter 3

A New Career Path

*Undertaking a PhD: The
Doctor Will See You Now!*

Dr Christopher Wilson

Introduction by Luke Beardon

It is a fantastic achievement to be awarded a
doctorate. I am fortunate in that I have the honour
of supervising students at doctoral level and I
am of the opinion that students with Asperger's
syndrome (AS) can make superb candidates for
higher degree engagement. Originality of thought,
ability to focus on one area of study for prolonged
periods of time, clarity of argument, passion for
a subject, depth of thinking, solitary study...these
are all aspects of what might be needed for a PhD
and, by wonderful coincidence, are often strong
attributes found in people with AS. It seems to
me that, in fact, doctoral study may offer less
of a challenge to some individuals with AS than
previous academic undertakings. The doctorate can
'allow' for a more individual way of working, the
student has more ownership, it is traditionally not
examined in ways that other awards are, group work
is not usually a part of the process, supervisions
can be held at times suited to the student – it could
be argued that a PhD is more 'AS-friendly' than
academic study of other kinds. Many people with

AS struggle educationally – not through lack of ability, but as a result of the constraints of teaching and learning within mainstream environments. It might be worth bearing in mind, though, that if one can achieve at school/college/university, then the doctoral route might be a more pleasant and achievable goal than ever imagined.

A surprising choice

At college, I found that when operating in a more adult environment and not forced to undertake subjects which I had no interest in or aptitude for (sport, of course, but also in my case, maths) I was able to better focus on the work in question and perform well.

I found that I had a good aptitude for geography, and essay writing generally (I also studied history). At the end of the course it was generally assumed that students would either become a local authority planner (i.e. someone who assesses planning applications for new development, or the modification of existing buildings, or who writes the policies that guide the decisions of other planners) or a private planning consultant (who submits planning applications to local authorities on behalf of private clients). This is the career path I assumed that I would be taking right up to the end of the course. Indeed, in early 2002 I had begun to apply to the graduate intake programmes of some of the larger planning consultancy firms in Manchester. However, as I neared the end of my course I began to consider just how much I had enjoyed my time at Manchester University and how well I had fitted in there. Specific things that I enjoyed included:

- the lifestyle – the 'big city' environment

- the work – as I mentioned, essay writing is something I am quite good at

- managed socialising – i.e. for a fairly defined time period, with breaks in between; not too rowdy; and not interfering with periods of quality 'me time' when I could do my own thing.

It was my parents who gave me the initial idea of carrying on and undertaking a PhD.

Taking a risk

However, there was also quite a bit of risk in the idea. As I could not afford to fund myself for the three years it would take to get a doctorate, I would have to bid for grant money. In my discipline (in 2002 at least), this generally meant a submission to the Economic and Social Research Council (ESRC) for funds. This entailed writing a brief synopsis of the research I intended to do (which was looking into community involvement in a large housing redevelopment programme that was being undertaken at the time – the Housing Market Renewal Initiative (HMRi)) along with responses to several other questions. Submissions had to be completed in May and you would find out if you had been successful that following September.

I did this and thus, while most of my friends went out to get full-time jobs, I waited from May to September 2002 to find out my result. As you can imagine this was a risk – if I didn't get the money, I couldn't do the PhD and would have to get a job. However, I would have lost three months on the jobs market and would have missed out on the spring graduate intake that many of the larger consultancy firms operate. In the worst case scenario it could take me till the following winter to get my career back on track.

September 2002 came around and I awaited the letter that would decide my future. I had been told that when the result came (by post) a thick envelope meant good news (since it would, in addition to the letter, contain an ESRC handbook for students), while a thin envelope meant bad news (since it only contained a single rejection letter). So when the envelope arrived and my mum shouted up to me, I remember screaming 'Is it thick, is it thick!' Well it was thick(ish) and I had my funding – I was going back to uni as a doctoral student.

Positive experiences of a PhD
Being your own boss

For those of you who aren't familiar with what a PhD (doctorate) is, it is essentially a three-year single academic research project, i.e. you spend your three years assembling a hypothesis, testing that hypothesis and writing up your research. Very crudely, you spend your first year defining what you want to research and how you are going to research it (your methodology), your second year doing the research and your third year writing it all up.[1]

However, the important point is that it is all your own work, done by yourself from start to finish, in your own time, with only modest input from your PhD tutor and other lecturers.

Working to your own timetable can be difficult and a surprisingly large number of people struggle to keep the momentum going if there is no-one there to motivate them on a day-to-day basis. People also tend to think in short timescales so planning for deadlines that could be years in advance does not come naturally. Therefore, it is perhaps not surprising that despite having three years to complete the thesis (PhD document), or six years for those doing it on a part-time basis, several of my fellow doctoral students still failed to submit their theses within the timeframe.

However, I found that I thrived under such a working environment and was good at motivating myself to do at

---

1   Editors' note: this is just one example of a PhD journey – doctoral research is very individual and each student will progress differently dependent on a wide range of influencing factors.

least some work each day. The pace of work required was not heavy and I found that I could have quite leisurely mornings and then put in some five hours in the afternoon, five days a week, to meet my (self-appointed) deadlines. Indeed, I even found myself ahead of schedule on many occasions.

There were few set lectures/seminars I had to attend as a PhD student and, generally, I only had to drive into Manchester one day a week. Most of the rest of the time I (with exceptions I will talk about more below) was in my room, working at the computer alone or in the university library. Some may find this low level of day-to-day interaction with others difficult, but as someone who often finds socialising challenging (and always tiring), this was exactly where I wanted to be. Amongst other things, it allowed me to set up a reliable routine for my weekdays in terms of when I slept in until, where I went to lunch, how long I worked and so on. Generally, it also allowed me plenty of time to 'be myself' and get on with productive activities without being distracted by the need to make myself 'presentable' and meet the numerous expectations of society.

Getting to know my area

One thing that may seem odd to others is spending three years researching one single topic. Outside of academia there are few other circumstances where you would spend three years on one single project, to the exclusion of almost everything else. However, this was another aspect that I found enjoyable – focusing on one issue, addressing one problem brought out the obsessive that I find in myself (and is doubtless found in many others with AS). Much of my research focused around three case study locations in East Lancashire, and in each I was able to get to know the area, the people, the local environment and local problems and issues.

In the town of Nelson, Pendle, I got to know and interview a group opposing the housing clearance planned there.

In Bacup, Rossendale, I attended the monthly meetings of the local community group, while in Burnley I interviewed local councillors and other community leaders.

Everyone was friendly, approachable and eager to talk. It helped that I had chosen to research one of the smaller HMRi programmes. Much larger schemes were also being undertaken in major northern cities like Manchester, Liverpool, Leeds, Sheffield, Hull and Newcastle, and these were grabbing all the headlines and academic interest. The people of East Lancashire felt ignored by comparison and happy that at least one person seemed to be taking an interest.

Teaching and academic experience

Teaching is not something I ever imagined I would be doing prior to starting my PhD. Certainly I had had few (positive) experiences with public speaking prior to that point and little confidence as a public speaker. So it is understandable that lecturing is one aspect of academic life that I did not rush to embrace. However, although I wasn't looking forward to it, I knew I should try and gain some teaching experience during the three years to prepare me for my (probable) academic future. It was therefore a very pleasant surprise to find out that when I was able to talk in a structured way, with plenty of preparation beforehand, I could speak knowledgably and confidently about the subject at hand. I wasn't perfect certainly; like many with AS, I can't think quickly and a difficult question could easily catch me unawares. However, if I knew my subject and could speak before an adult audience, I found that I could master this previously unknown skill. In addition to leading several student seminars I presented papers at several large planning and geography conferences in London and Reading, and assisted on an undergraduate residential trip to Holland in my final year.

In addition to this I worked as a research assistant for several lecturers during the three-year course. Usually, only working one day a week, this added some diversity to my weekly routine by letting me become involved in other academics' projects. Again my ability to work quietly, quickly and with a minimum of distraction helped me be an asset to the lecturers, turning some of my AS 'negatives' (i.e. obsessiveness, limited social life, unwillingness to look beyond my own world) into positives as a hard, accurate and prolific worker. Among the many things I achieved as a research assistant was to add my name to several published articles and one edited book chapter.

Socialising

Although I tried (and usually succeeded) in keeping a steady pace of work going, being my own boss did give me the freedom to occasionally do something 'spontaneous' like see a mid-week movie, go for a long walk or see a friend. Having a routine is a good thing but adding some occasional variety to that routine can also help make life more interesting and more enjoyable. I had the freedom to see friends when I wanted but also the freedom to keep that socialising to 'bite sized chunks', which I could cope with and which still left me with plenty of time for rest and recuperation. This approach certainly seemed to work well; indeed it helped me stay friends with two individuals from my undergraduate course despite the fact that those two went on to have separate careers, get married and (in one case) have children.

My new future

Generally, I had three positive years working towards my doctorate. It was not all perfect of course; during that period my grandmother passed away. I also had at least one major crisis of confidence towards the end of my third year as I began to grapple with the deeper aspects of academic theory. However, after a few sleepless nights I was able to work the issues through with my PhD supervisor. I should also say that I was very lucky in that my supervisor was an extremely experienced (and patient!) older professor who was nearing retirement (he technically did retire while I was there) and was winding down his other commitments. He therefore had plenty of time to support my work and advise me through the PhD process.

The end result was that I was able to go on and gain my doctorate. The fact that I am now 'Dr Wilson' and have a string of other letters after my name still amazes me, particularly when I consider how much I struggled in early life. My PhD graduation ceremony in December 2006 (the third such ceremony I have attended!) was a great moment of pride for me, particularly as I was one of only six doctoral students graduating that day, compared to some 500 undergraduate and postgraduate students. The robes you get to wear as a PhD graduate are a lot nicer than the undergraduate/ postgrad robes as well!

In addition to writing my PhD thesis (a mere 100,000 words plus appendices!) I was able to get articles published in several journals, planning magazines and one edited book. Writing these helped me improve my writing style and was a great confidence booster in my ability to create works that would be accepted by a professional audience, even if I did also have some articles rejected.

Ultimately, I did not carry on into academia after graduation. I had had a great three years, but experience had taught me that I was still more of a practical and vocational thinker than an academic one. I had struggled with the more theoretical aspects of my subject and it seemed likely that this would become more of an issue if I carried on to undertake post-doctoral research.

However, having determined not to carry on into academia, completing my PhD did give me the confidence to look at more varied and diverse career options than I otherwise would have, had I gone into practice straight from my undergraduate course. Being Dr Wilson looked very good on the CV as well! As an example, I first looked at a number of planning posts in unusual locations including the Orkney Islands and Auckland, New Zealand. However, I ultimately settled on a more local job with a company that specialises in research work for local authorities. While not in a particularly exotic location (Warrington!) the work is extremely diverse, in fields such as economic development and urban regeneration, and provides me with regular challenges (and crises!), which I feel better able to cope with after three years of PhD research work.

Lessons for those with AS
It can take time to understand your future

I was a late bloomer who struggled in school, both socially and academically. It wasn't till I moved on to A levels and particularly undergraduate university studies that I found a passion and an aptitude for learning, when I could focus on subjects of interest and work in a more 'adult' environment. Since then my life has taken several unpredictable turns as I moved to undertake my PhD and then moved on to the very different world of professional practice. I could not have predicted either of those changes more than a couple of months before they happened.

It took me a while to understand my future and just what my capabilities were – an experience that many who read this book will be able to relate to. A bad experience at school, or in childhood generally, need not define a person for the rest of their lives. And just because you are stuck in a bad job, bad relationship or bad domestic situation now does not mean it will always be so. A change in environment, in lifestyle or maybe in something simple, like diet, may help you discover a new and positive aspect of yourself.

Taking risks is part of life

The common perception is that those with AS are fairly 'risk averse' individuals. There may be some truth in this, although another way of looking at it is to argue that those with AS take more 'risks' in their daily lives – in engaging with society, in starting a conversation which may go wrong, in entering environments they are unprepared for – than others ever do. When I applied for my PhD I had to take a big risk in bidding for my funding, and waiting a whole summer for the result. Had I failed, my future career plans would have taken a big knock and it would have taken me a while to get back on track.

The lesson here is that risk is part of life for everyone and, unfortunately, even more so for those with AS. To get ahead, to develop as a person, or simply to go about your daily life requires accepting some risks. This can be hard to accept, but if you do, it can help reduce your day-to-day stress and worry. And when you do take a risk, and it pays off, it can be a great feeling.

Socialising – know your strengths and limitations

I have never felt that those with AS are anti-social, but we do generally like to socialise on our own terms, in ways we are comfortable with. For someone with AS there can be few, day-to-day experiences worse than being trapped in an awkward social encounter where you can't (and maybe don't want to) engage with those round you.

Among other benefits, my PhD helped me understand my strengths and limitations in terms of social interaction. In terms of strengths I discovered that I could be a reasonable public speaker as long as I knew my topic, had practised in advance and was not asked any difficult or unexpected questions. I can also be quite confident at approaching new people as long as I can see that there is little risk of being rejected.

In terms of limitations, I find that I can
with people for some three or four hours at a ti.
I need a break, some privacy or at least a period
also have quite a short attention span and my min.
to wander if people tell me a story that doesn't immedi.
interest me. In recent years, I have also discovered th.
engaging with people through social media is not a particular
skill of mine.

Some of you might find the above statements familiar;
some might have very different strengths and limitations
– for example, preferring social media encounters to face-
to-face interactions. However, whatever your personal
preferences, it is important to learn what methods of
social interaction suit you best and how you can be most
comfortable in dealing with others, in order to get the
most out of life.

Have a routine and (occasionally) break it

One of the benefits of my PhD work was that during the three
years in which I undertook my PhD I was able to build up
quite a strong routine – getting up at the same time, eating
at the same places, working for the same amount of time.
Having a clear routine in life can be very comforting, but
there is often a fine line between having a strong routine and
being obsessive about things. It is all too common to hear
those with AS state that they cannot possibly survive without
doing this or that activity, at a certain time, when the activity
often seems unimportant or irrelevant to outsiders.

It is therefore equally important to occasionally break
a routine and try something new. 'Trying something new'
could be as simple as changing the foods you eat, the time
you take a shower, going out for a meal, going for a day out
or taking a longer holiday. Being willing to break routines
can open you up to new experiences, new understandings
of the world and engaging with people in it. This is certainly

one way to find new positive experiences and improve your general mental health.

Build up new skills in life

Doing a PhD certainly helped me develop new skills, or at least build up existing ones. During those three years I lectured, managed classes of undergraduates, spoke at conferences, wrote academic papers and undertook a whole range of other things I would never have imagined myself doing under other circumstances. We develop as individuals by learning new skills and experiencing new things. Not everything we try will be successful but we can also learn from our failures.

Do something that interests you

I stuck with my PhD for three years (plus five years of other university courses before that) because I was doing something that interested and excited me. This allowed me to motivate myself to work five days a week when there was no-one around to supervise me on a day-to-day basis. As individuals it is important to have at least one thing in our lives that interests us and helps motivate us to get on with the less interesting aspects of our daily lives. This could be your job, but could also be a hobby, pet, friendship or relationship.

People often talk about the weaknesses of those with AS, but one of the often ignored strengths is the ability to find a hobby or interest independent of others. Those with AS, as a general rule, don't need to be 'entertained' by others all the time and have the focus to find an activity that is special to them as individuals. If you do not already have such an activity that 'gets you up in the morning', then try and find one – it could be just the positive experience you need.

Chapter 4

Becoming a Parent Is Really, Really Hard... Who Would Have Guessed?

Becky Heaver

Introduction by Luke Beardon

This is a gorgeous piece of writing that captures so much of the emotional depths of parenting; it is also a superb insight into the perspective of a mum with Asperger's syndrome (AS). Becky's articulation of how she acknowledges her strengths as a person with AS and utilises them to ensure she does the best for her daughter is uplifting – and perfectly ties in with the positive theme of this collation of chapters. I have met women with AS who have told me that they would be scared to disclose their AS in case people would then think them unfit mothers – how horrendous would it be to be in that position, to feel that people's understanding of AS would lead them to such a conclusion? Having AS will almost invariably make a difference to how one parents a child; Becky's writing makes it clear that in her case it can be a very positive difference indeed.

I gave birth to my daughter earlier this year, and after a challenging start, she's now four months old and pretty amazing. It's quite honestly the hardest thing I've ever done. Not hard like the struggles of daily living with Asperger's syndrome can be, it's a different kind of hard: something I've entered into out of choice and therefore feel somewhat in control of; something that I get a lot out of in return for all the effort; and definitely a situation which I don't want to change, because it's also the best thing I've ever done.

My partner (who already has three children) takes great delight in telling me every day how he said it was going to be really hard, and that he told me I was going to find it difficult. A mixture of 'I've done this before' smugness, and 'I don't know when to wind my neck in' Aspie-ness. I've tried to explain to him that there was no way he, or anybody, could have prepared me for what it was going to be like, and how I was going to feel. I have great difficulty in imagining situations or states of being that I have not previously experienced, and in reality sometimes even imagining ones I have experienced, if they were not very recent. It got me thinking as to what he would have needed to say to me to try and convey a little bit of my current reality, particularly those first few weeks with a tiny, helpless, newborn baby, and it went something like this:

You've just had your heart broken, and fallen in love, at the same time. You've come down with really bad flu and been beaten up, but you feel really wonderful and alive. You're trapped in a real-life game of *The Sims* where there's never enough time, and just when you've made an action plan, something more urgent crops up and you have to start all over again – but without the benefit of 'Save and Quit' when you've had enough. You don't get time to breathe, and have to make choices between eating and using the toilet, or end up eating whilst using the toilet, just to catch up with yourself. Your sense of personal hygiene is plumbing new depths of scuddiness, and friends are starting to wonder if you only own one outfit (rather than the veritable fashion parade of the three rotating outfits that you normally wear). Life becomes a rather strange contrast of lovely and horrible, competence and doubt, pride and guilt. You find yourself longing for the future when you assume things will be easier, but at the same time savouring every moment because you know you will never get this time back. You take more photos than you will ever be able to show anybody, because you can't bear to miss a single minute of her growing and developing, and becoming her own little person. I think that even if somebody had told me all that, it still wouldn't have captured the personal changes I have noticed. My feelings for my daughter are so strong that I actually recognise and can articulate them. I put her first without hesitation, and somehow find the motivation to do what she needs me to do, even on days when I can't manage to do basic things for myself. She's become my mission, my purpose in life, my everything – a concept that wasn't even on my radar before I had her. News items or documentaries about children make me blub like only cartoons and animals could before. Hormones (and analgesics) have coloured the memory of my labour so pink and rosy, to the point where I even miss it with nostalgic sadness. Had you told that to the pre-baby me, even the pregnant me, the one who was so terrified of giving birth that I delayed having children until I was 35, I would have laughed in your face so hard that I probably would have spittled a little.

Whilst I often struggle with some basic parenting staples such as multitasking, knowing how to talk to other children (or parents for that matter), attending baby groups without crying, putting fashionable outfits together without step-by-step guides or understanding how to 'play' and make up stories, I like to think that I also bring some pretty hefty Aspie strengths to the mix. My memory is terrible, therefore I already have to be super-organised with lots of lists, diaries and reminders, so slotting baby-related appointments or 'to-do' items into those is no effort at all. Kids need routine? Well duh! I can do routine (and ritual – because family traditions are good for children's resilience and well-being) with my eyes shut. I understand what sensory overload is like, and how to help her when she gets over-stimulated. If she has special interests, these will be encouraged and nurtured, even if they are different to my own (although dance lessons will be compulsory obviously). Keeping up to date with the latest parenting information? Babies (well my baby at least) are my new special interest, so I've probably already read it, read a couple of critiques and made some notes in my baby journal before it's even made it onto the Baby Centre website. Not to mention a desire to buy lots of Lego and play with it, for her benefit of course… It will be a while yet before I know whether my daughter is on the spectrum too, like her dad and I, and if I'm completely honest, a part of me would really like her to share our world, as long as we can make her journey there easier than ours were. In contrast to my late diagnosis and years of being misunderstood, whatever her neurodiversity or otherwise, I will make sure that she experiences the kind of non-judgemental acceptance that is so critical for positive self-image, -esteem and -confidence, and support her happiness, whoever and whatever she grows up to be.

Chapter 5

Autism and Music

Michael Barton

Introduction by Luke Beardon

Michael's passion for music comes through strongly within his writing; he also provides some excellent examples of how music has played a positive role in the lives of others. Of course, music can be a passion for anyone, and play a positive role in the lives of a person whether they are autistic or not – but what is very clear and extremely well articulated by Michael is the way in which music can provide a natural conduit of interaction between a person with Asperger's syndrome (AS) and his peers. Universality is not something that can be easily discovered for many people, but Michael demonstrates just how universal music is with several examples of his own experiences. As Michael so brilliantly demonstrates, sometimes all it takes to bridge that gap between people is a shared interest. I think that many people on the spectrum don't like the 'spotlight' when interacting; it can be so stressful having to 'say the right thing' and constantly worrying about 'getting it wrong'. With a focus on the shared interest, it may be that the 'spotlight' moves away from the person and onto the subject, which might provide some relief to the individual. It certainly seems to have worked in a very positive way for Michael!

About the writer

Michael Barton is a physics graduate with high-functioning autism. He has written and illustrated two books, entitled *It's Raining Cats and Dogs* (2011) and *A Different Kettle of Fish* (2014), published by Jessica Kingsley Publishers, and is a regular and experienced speaker focusing on the positive aspects of autism. In this chapter he will explain why music has been such an important part of his life – he's an accomplished musician, playing piano, bass guitar, drums, percussion and spoons. He also explains how it has helped him develop into the confident and able individual he is today.

The beginning

I was fortunate to grow up in a musical household. My dad would play guitar and sing us nursery rhymes literally every day, and he also played in a band (with my mum on drums!). I started formal piano lessons when I was eight. I had a strict schedule of piano practice right from the start and it quickly became part of my daily routine. One reason why I kept up my practice was probably because of my autistic traits, i.e. liking routine and repetition, so in this respect autism actually proved to be an advantage. So many people have said to me 'I wish I'd kept up my music practice', but they didn't have the same focus and willpower that autistic people often exhibit.

Having an appropriate teacher, who was actually a Special Educational Needs (SEN) teacher with a good understanding of autism, helped a lot. She didn't take offence when I appeared rude or blunt and allowed me to progress at my own rate.

Playing piano, or in fact any instrument, is a good way to chill out for autistic people. Coping with the overwhelming social demands of everyday life meant that having half an hour to myself without disturbance every day was very much welcomed. I didn't have to worry about anyone or anything else. It was just me and the piano.

By the time I was 11 I was good enough to play piano with my parents' band, and I still remember my first ever gig at a local social club. By the age of 13 I was playing with them in pubs, but usually had to leave after the first half because of school the next day!

School

I was never going to make many friends at school with my below par social skills, however I found that my musical ability was starting to be admired by my peers. Joining bands at school helped me socialise and my secondary school had a very good music department with (almost) soundproof studios. This meant that I didn't have to spend my lunch time out in the playground (which was difficult with few friends and poor social skills) – instead I was able to go to one of these rooms and practise at lunch time.

One unfortunate incident that I had during the summer holidays, aged ten, was when I was bouncing around the garden on a space hopper and fell off backwards. I put my hand out to save myself but broke a finger on my right hand! My initial reaction was 'Oh, I can't do any piano practice without my right hand' (after the pain subsided of course), but my parents replied that I would have to practise with just my left hand for six weeks. I duly obliged, seeing the logic behind this, and still practised every day, which actually really helped develop and build up the muscles in my left hand. Normally a right-handed player has a much stronger right hand but after six weeks I'd closed the gap. Having a strong left hand is essential for many pieces, particularly when playing stride piano, rock 'n' roll and boogie woogie. My sister actually once said, 'I wish I'd broken a finger in my right hand so that I could have a strong left hand too!' (Today she has an associate diploma in piano and studies music at Bristol University.)

My secondary school regularly held informal concerts – an evening dedicated to students where anyone could get up on stage and play a piece. This was a great opportunity for me. I would work very hard to get a piece perfect for these concerts – I especially enjoyed pieces like 'The Maple Leaf Rag' and 'The Entertainer' by Scott Joplin, extravaganzas like 'Handful of Keys' by Fats Waller (which really is a handful!) and Winnifred Atwell's 'Black and White Rag'. This exposed my skills to my peers, which made me more interesting to them (instead of just being this weird kid who was a bit different). Temple Grandin, probably the most famous autistic person in the world, says, 'People appreciate talent and being good at something helps compensate for being weird.'[1]

Once I reached grade 7 classical piano, which I got the day after my 14th birthday, I wanted to move onto jazz, as I found the pieces more exciting. We got the grade 7 jazz syllabus book and showed it to my piano teacher, but she took one look at it and said, 'I can't teach this! The scales are all different and there are huge gaps in the set pieces where you're supposed to improvise!' This resulted in me having to find a new teacher, which was a concern as she had understood me so well.

Another reason why this was a potential issue is that autistic people are known for strongly disliking change in their lives. I have, however, learned that things don't always stay the same and we therefore need to embrace change, as change can actually lead to the situation improving.

We were fortunate to find another great teacher who was a brilliant jazz pianist who happened to have an autistic son. Also, his musical 'ancestry' actually went back to Beethoven, as shown below:

---

1   Grandin, T. (2008) *The Way I See it: A Personal Look at Autism and Asperger's*. Arlington, TX: Future Horizons, Inc., p.228.

Ludvig Van Beethoven (1770–1827)

taught

Carl Czerny (1791–1857)

taught

Theodor Leschetizky (1830–1915)

taught

Mabel Lander (1882–1955)

taught

James Gibbs (1918–2013)

taught

Maxim Rowlands (1958–)

taught

Michael Barton (1992–)

I had to go right back to grade 5 again because jazz is so different. I then progressed onto grade 8 jazz piano, which I passed with a distinction. I wish to stress at this point that it is vitally important to find a teacher with a good understanding of autism as it can make all the difference.

When I was in sixth form the school announced that they were going to put on a Monty Python show. Since I knew the piano to Monty Python's 'Not the Noel Coward Song' (a rather rude song performed by Eric Idle in *The Meaning of Life*, part 6, 'The Autumn Year'). I was keen to participate, so I asked the organiser if I could do it and he said, 'I suppose we could get away with it.' I'd always planned to play this at the leaver's concert, once all my exams were over and they couldn't do anything to punish me, but the Monty Python evening was such a good opportunity I had to take it. So I performed this song in front of a large audience, including the headmaster (and his mother, who wasn't too happy with it!) but this was a great way of gaining some popularity and respect from my peers.

University

The University of Surrey was a fantastic opportunity for me to join a variety of music clubs and meet lots of new people with similar musical interests who I could thus talk to and get on with. I joined the jazz orchestra playing piano, and concert band and wind orchestra playing French horn. Another music-related club I joined in my final year was called 'No Wave' (the alternative music society), which was yet another great way for me to meet people with a common interest.

This is one of the brilliant things about university – you're studying a subject you are passionate about and can join any club you wish, or even set one up provided you find enough people also willing to do so. You also get some quite obscure clubs at university, which can be ideal for someone on the spectrum. Where else would you find a cheese appreciation society or *Doctor Who* society? It's also particularly easy to get involved, as people in societies and clubs welcome new members.

One of the other clubs that I joined was the rock climbing club. Strangely enough there were a lot of physicists and engineers in the club, some with more autistic traits than others! In my opinion it's easy to see why this is – it takes dedication and perseverance (something all autistic people have a lot of when it comes to something they're passionate about) to complete a particular route on the climbing wall and people can get quite obsessive over one specific move. It turns out these skills are very similar to those required to become proficient in a musical instrument.

Over the Easter holidays in my first year the club went on a rock climbing trip to Cornwall. One night we all decided to go to the local pub and there was a live skiffle band playing that evening. I was intrigued by the instrument the lead guy was playing – it looked halfway between a banjo and a ukulele. So I went up to him in the interval to ask him what it was – a banjulele as it turns out. I told him I was a musician and that I played the spoons and he was very keen for me to play with the band for a couple of songs in the second half, including a couple of solos. This totally amazed my rock climbing friends, none of whom had the slightest idea that I was a musician. After my performance everyone wanted to talk to me and bombarded me with questions and praise – I was probably the most popular person in the pub that night! If this isn't a good example of using my musical skills to oil the wheels of social interaction and make friends, I don't know what is!

At this point I should mention that I have been taught the spoons by probably the best spoons player in the world, the hugely talented and famous Sam Spoons of the legendary Bonzo Dog Doo Dah Band.

Michael having his spoons lesson with Sam Spoons

At a gig I did a few months later, after a particularly virtuoso spoons performance, an audience member came up to me and said, 'Wow! You really are the Jimi Hendrix of spoons, aren't you?!'

When I give my presentations about the positive aspects of autism I relate the story of playing spoons in the pub as an example of how I've been able to overcome social difficulties by using my skills and strengths. I finish my presentations by giving the audience a spoons demonstration, which is the last thing they expect because autism talks usually focus on the difficulties autistic people face and the negatives of the condition. The audience is always amazed, which means they go away uplifted, inspired and with a positive frame of mind. When I give talks to pupils at schools, the most common question I get at the end is 'Can you play the spoons again?' It certainly means they remember me and hopefully start to realise that autism can have many positives and is not all doom and gloom by any means.

Going back to my degree in physics, I believe that there is a link between music and science. Einstein was actually an accomplished violinist and pianist and once said, 'If I were not a physicist I would have been a musician.'[2] Music was a form of relaxation for Einstein, yet it also served as an inspiration and helped in his work. It also seemed to be the driving force behind his entire creative process. His son, Hans Albert Einstein, recalls his father using music as a tool to help him with his work: 'Whenever he felt that he had come to the end of the road or into a difficult situation in his work, he would take refuge in music. That would usually resolve all his difficulties.'[3]

I've found it surprisingly common for people to be good at maths and music – there is definitely a mathematical element to music, especially when it comes down to the timing, frequencies, harmonics and rhythm. Many autistic children have above average mathematical abilities, and the same can be said about music. Kanner, who first described

2   From 'What Life Means to Einstein: An Interview by George Sylvester Viereck.' *The Saturday Evening Post* (26 October 1929), p.17.

3   Clark, R. W. (1971) *Einstein: The Life and Times*. New York: The World Publishing Company, p.106.

autism in 1943, described several examples of extraordinary musical memory in his clinical group. In fact 6 of the 11 case studies he describes exhibited music-related behaviours far above those expected for their developmental levels. I believe that music should therefore be encouraged and every opportunity given to autistic children to pursue musical interests.

Another musical event at university was the annual talent competition, 'Surrey's Got Talent'. This was another opportunity to show people my spoon playing ability. In my last year I got through to the final and performed in front of a hall of 200 people! People then came up to me afterwards saying 'I've never seen anything like that before!' and for the next few days people would randomly stop me on campus and start up conversations. It really is good to have a skill like this that people appreciate.

The third year of my degree was spent on an industrial placement, where I worked full time for a year in a science park at the Brunel Innovation Centre in Cambridge. I didn't know anybody in Cambridge but got on well with my colleagues as they were scientifically minded as well. About halfway through the year I went to a pub one night with a friend, where we coincidentally saw a live band. This turned out to be part of a blues jam session (when a group of people go on stage and play a few songs, then the line up changes and different people from the audience go and play). Having played bass guitar for a number of years, and because of the fact that I very much enjoy blues music, I had a go on bass that night and was hooked. They asked me to come back the following week and, for the rest of my year there, I went every week. They welcomed me each time, letting me go on stage a couple of times every night, and I was even invited to play some gigs with another band I met there who needed a bassist when theirs was on holiday.

Michael playing at a jam night

I have since found out about jam sessions local to where I live and go to them on a weekly basis. This is a fantastic way to meet new people and wherever my next job will take me I know exactly how I can find people to play music with and make new friends.

Once you're good at one instrument, it's much easier to pick up another. This is the main reason why I've been able to pick up multiple instruments and why only one lesson on bass guitar was sufficient to get me started (I knew what I wanted to play, I just needed to learn how to operate the instrument). I've also learned drums, washboard and various other percussion instruments, thanks to my musical ability and very strong sense of rhythm.

To this day I still perform with my family band, doing fundraising gigs for local charities (including two autistic charities that have helped me). It's great to see the audience so involved and enjoying themselves. I go to jam sessions twice a week and I still practise often and always have a new piece on the go.

When I look back on my life, I can see that music has not just been a hobby or extracurricular activity at school for me, but has also been an essential part in every area of my life. I strongly believe music can be enriching for many other people too. Music, either instrumental or vocal, can be learnt by anybody at any age. There are now so many different ways in which you can learn a musical instrument – having lessons, YouTube, CDs, etc. – that there's bound to be something for you.

Looking back/how music has helped me
Overcoming social difficulties

Music is a great way of making friends without needing to have great social skills. You don't need to initiate conversation as the music does the talking. I've found that people come up to me and want to talk to me after I've performed on stage.

Stress buster

Playing music is a perfect example of focusing on the here and now, and is a great stress buster and form of relaxation. Many autistic people display higher levels of anxiety than the majority of the population. Most anxiety is caused by worrying about what's happened in the past or what's going to happen in the future, and music is one way to help temporarily forget about all of that and appreciate the moment you're in. As described by Therese Jolliffe, 'When I am feeling angry and despairing of everything, music is the only way of making me feel calmer inside.'[4]

---

4   Jolliffe, T. and Baron-Cohen, S. (1999) 'A test of central coherence theory: linguistic processing in high-functioning adults with autism or Asperger syndrome: is local coherence impaired.' *Cognition 71*, 149–185. Available at http://docs.autismresearchcentre. com/papers/1999_Jolliffe_BC_Cognition.pdf, accessed 23 October 2016, p.15.

Emotional regulator

Music provides an outlet for autistic people to convey emotion as well as potentially a way to understand emotions: According to Adam Ockelford, a professor of music, 'Music provides important intellectual and emotional nourishment...essential brain food for children on the autistic spectrum.'[5] As an autistic adult in the Allen *et al.* (2009) study said:[6]

> I find that sometimes if you're feeling very sad or something, listening to that kind of music can put you in touch with your feelings, it can help you to access your feelings. You can really feel the feelings instead of their just being there, you can really dwell in that state and deal with it.

Developing confidence and presentation skills

Most neurotypical people, let alone autistic people, aren't able to stand up in front of an audience, or feel very self-conscious and anxious doing so. Thanks to the hundreds of performances I've done, plus the knowledge that I'm an accomplished musician and good at what I do, I'm quite happy to do so. Stage fright disappears with practice! I'm sure music has also given me confidence to achieve in other areas of my life – music can enhance learning in general. If I can perform so well on the piano, then I know I have the ability to accomplish other goals in my life.

Helping to learn to read body language

Playing music with other people means you have to learn how to read their cues and be ready for any signals they

---

5   Ockelford, A. (2013) *Music, Language and Autism: Exceptional Strategies for Exceptional Minds.* London: Jessica Kingsley Publishers, p.260.

6   Allen, R., Hill, E. and Heaton, P. (2009) '"Hath charms to soothe...": an exploratory study of how high-functioning adults with ASD experience music.' *Autism 13,* 1, 21–41.

might give you. Even though autistic people often don't appreciate or can't read body language, music forces you to use body language as there's no other way to communicate in the middle of a song.

Special interest

A special interest is an intense interest, or obsession, with a specific topic. It's rare to find an autistic person without a special interest. Music is a great special interest to get into because everybody likes music, in some form or another. According to Francesca Happé, a professor of cognitive neuroscience, 'Music is a space where people with autism spectrum conditions and neurotypicals can truly meet.'[7]

The same can't be said about other special interests that autistic people often get absorbed in (such as washing machines or batteries), but music is truly a universal language.

Suggestions to help others

Learn a musical instrument

I would highly recommend parents to encourage their child to learn to play a musical instrument, or autistic people themselves to take up an instrument (it doesn't matter what age you are – as long as you put quality hours in, you're going to get good). It has played such an important part in my life that I cannot recommend it enough.

Practise every day

Even if it's just 15 minutes a day, the hours will all add up – it's better to do 15 minutes a day than two hours once a week. Autistic people very much like to have a fixed routine in their lives, so practising an instrument on a daily basis with a schedule gives them this sense of security. They know

---

7   Ockelford, A. (2013) *Music, Language and Autism: Exceptional Strategies for Exceptional Minds*. London: Jessica Kingsley Publishers, p.9.

what's going to happen and when it's going to happen. They also like repetition in their lives, so learning to play a musical instrument, which requires both routine and repetition, means autistic people can use these traits to their advantage.

Get involved in clubs

Joining clubs is a great way of sharing common interests and making friends. Autistic people are very happy to talk about something they're interested in and if you're in a club, and therefore talking to someone also interested in the subject, the other person will be happy to listen (unlike many parents!). Social and communication skills will then develop as a byproduct.

Find opportunities to perform

I was lucky to have regular opportunities to perform pieces to an audience. Having informal concerts at school, for example, was not only a great motivator to learn new pieces but it also gave me invaluable experience performing in front of an audience, boosting confidence and self-esteem.

The opportunity to perform can be life changing. Susan Boyle, a contestant on *Britain's Got Talent*, who was diagnosed with Asperger's syndrome in 2013 aged 52, said:

> Music seems to be my medication. It seems to make me feel better. When I'm up on stage, even if I've had a bad day, I can become a different person. I feel safe. Why? I don't feel judged up there. I feel accepted.[8]

Keep motivated

It is vitally important to keep yourself motivated when learning a musical instrument. Playing should be a hobby and therefore enjoyable; it must not feel like a chore. This

---

8   From an interview with Jenny Johnston: 'The truth about my Asperger's: Susan Boyle reveals just how difficult it is living with a condition that makes her behaviour so very unpredictable.' *The Daily Mail* (14 November 2014).

is where the teacher's role is important – scales may appear boring but are essential in learning proper technique and working on dexterity. Another important point is to constantly keep the end goal in mind, reminding yourself why you're practising in the first place. This in turn will help overcome change and other difficult situations.

Afterword

One of my heroes, not surprisingly as I'm a physicist, is Albert Einstein, who clearly displayed many autistic traits. It seems clear that music played a big part in his life as well. He once said, 'I know that the most joy in my life has come to me from my violin.'[9]

Music also helped him socially, particularly when it came to attracting women. According to Elsa, his wife, 'I fell in love with Albert because he played Mozart so beautifully on the violin. I was so entranced by the beautiful melodies that I could hardly take my eyes off of him.'[10]

Well if it was good enough for Einstein, it's certainly good enough for me.

9   From 'What Life Means to Einstein: An Interview by George Sylvester Viereck.' *The Saturday Evening Post* (26 October 1929), p.17.

10   Pais, A. (2005) *Subtle is the Lord: The Science and the Life of Albert Einstein.* New York: Oxford University Press, p.301.

Chapter 6

How Discovering Creative Writing Opened Up a Whole New World for the Aspie in Me

Andrew Smith

Introduction by Luke Beardon

Andrew provides an excellent chapter around how he has taken a risk and it has paid off. It is difficult for many people with Asperger's syndrome (AS) to 'expose' themselves to new experiences, especially when those experiences include lots of 'new' people to meet and greet. However, choosing an activity where the focus is on a product (in this case writing) rather more than on the individual might be a very positive way of expanding social time and getting positive feedback. Very often when an individual – proactively or by chance – comes across an activity that they can share with others and focus on it in a positive way (hurray for Minecraft; of course it's not for everyone but I do know plenty of people on the spectrum for whom Minecraft has opened up all sorts of positive social opportunities), they can find it a rewarding experience. As Andrew demonstrates, there are pros and cons to all activities, but with careful consideration a chosen activity can be a catalyst not only to positive new developments in talents or skills, but also to new acquaintances and relationships.

January 2014 was a difficult month for me. I was sitting at home on my own, it was dark and cold outside and I was staring at a computer screen. I was depressed. I had no motivation, no physical or mental energy, no reason to even get up from my chair, there was nothing at all. As I sat there I thought to myself, 'I cannot go on like this, I need to do something, I need to change my life and soon.' I knew deep down that I couldn't go on like this. I felt as if I were being eaten from the inside out and slowly being devoured by my own lack of motivation and spirit for life. I knew I needed to change my life and soon!

So I decided I needed a hobby, an interest to complement my university studies and to keep my mind occupied, an outlet for my imagination free from the constraints of university studies. Whatever it was I decided to pursue as a hobby it had to be able to fit in with my studies though, as these are very important to me and especially for my future.

People had always told me I have a talent for writing, although what people meant by talent I didn't know. It wasn't anything I could quantify and put a number on to clarify the concept in my mind and have a mental picture of what talent is. It was and and still is something I feel is a very subjective concept, and one person's idea of talent is very different to someone else's as I have found out. So although I found the idea of talent to be a very abstract concept, in my mind I decided I had nothing to lose and set about looking for somewhere where I could see if I had any writing talent.

My first priority was to find a suitable group close to where I live as I don't like to travel too far or to areas that I am unfamiliar with. I did an internet search and found a local writing group called 'Igniting the Spark'. I nervously emailed the organiser and arranged to go down to my very first writing workshop. I was nervous and apprehensive as I arrived for my very first workshop but there was also a touch of excitement too as I entered the building and went looking for the room. I turned up early that first night as I didn't want to get lost or go into a room full of unfamiliar faces and fall apart.

Turning up early was a very good idea, though, and I was the first person there, which helped to settle my nerves. I was able to find a suitable seat and arrange my pens and paper. The organiser is a young lady called Gaia Holmes, and being the first person meant I was able to have a quick 'get to know you' chat and find out the format of the workshop before anyone else arrived, which helped to calm my nerves tremendously.

And then the others began to arrive, all huffing and puffing after a long day at work and a stressful journey rushing through rush hour traffic to get to the workshop! This too helped to calm me down as I realised that it wasn't just me who was stressed and anxious but others too, albeit for different reasons. We proceeded to get coffee and biscuits and then it was time to knuckle down to the reason why we had come here. To write!

Gaia gave us a sheet of paper each with some poems on. We took turns in reading a poem and although it was my first time there I decided to go for it and read rather than put it off. Once the readings had finished we gave our thoughts on the poems. The first exercise of the night was based on our own interpretation of the poems we had just read and I just sat there in a daze wondering what to do.

We spent around ten minutes writing a piece of poetry and it was a relief when the time was up. Gaia told us to stop and finish what we had written, and then asked the question 'Who wants to read their poem?', which can be a nerve wracking moment for most people and even more so for someone with Asperger's syndrome! I immediately put my hand up, again thinking to 'go for it and get it out of the way', and proceeded to read my very first attempt at poetry! To say I was nervous would be an understatement, but for one of the very first times in my life people were sitting around listening to me speak, to my words and not interrupting, walking away or looking at their mobile phones!

And to my complete surprise, people liked my poetry. People liked some words I had thought of from my own imagination and written on a blank piece of paper. They liked something I had created all on my own and it was just a very surreal experience for me but very enjoyable too. What surprised me even more was that they liked my voice and I sensed that they might even like me!

I was shocked and surprised at the response but in a nice way. Nobody was judging me on my appearance, my lack of social skills, my ability to get things wrong or to make things seem more complicated than they are. I was just being judged on the work I had produced, on a simple piece of poetry that took up maybe half a page of A4 and nothing more. This was a whole new experience for me, being thought of in this non-judgemental way.

Normally I perceive that I am judged on my physical appearance, my inability to read and accurately judge faces and body language, and my lack of control over my own facial expressions. When coupled with my lack of social skills, what I say or don't say and ability to say the wrong thing at the wrong time, this means that I spend most of my life worrying about what others think about me, rather than just getting on with life.

It was such a pleasant feeling being judged on something that I had produced, that I had created, that came from within my mind. And my writing journey didn't end there either. In fact it was just the beginning. I went back the next week and the week after and the week after that. In fact I still go to the writing workshop every week and I must admit it I miss it if I can't go as if my creativity is not getting its weekly dose of words to play with. But just as importantly for me I've made new friends too, hopefully friends for life; wonderful, caring people, genuine friends who are non-judgemental about my Asperger's and even say that it helps my writing because it gives it a different and unique flavour. For me this means I can leave my Asperger's outside and just be me for one evening a week.

But I was inspired to go further with my writing and decided to spread my wings further. I started to go to some poetry events where poets new and established, young and old, well known and unknown, read either their work or the work of famous poets to an appreciative audience. A poetry event is an experience in itself. The audience is as quiet as a church mouse as the poet performs.

This can be both good and bad. Good because you're not trying to filter out any background noise and you can concentrate on reading and performing. Bad because all you hear is your own voice and this can make you even more self-conscious because you hear your voice going up and down, fast and slow and every mistake you make! Your brain may be telling you one thing as you read and your eyes are darting all over the page trying to keep pace with your brain. I myself am very self-conscious when reading and often feel that I've messed up, but the feedback I get back is always very positive and heart-warming.

So what are the positives I have taken from writing? First, I find writing very therapeutic. In writing I have found a way of expressing my inner self and getting my thoughts and emotions out into the world. Even more importantly for me, writing is a way of getting myself heard that I never had before. When I am talking I often feel that I am not heard or understood and people either ignore me or talk over me.

With my writing I feel that I am heard and understood far more. I can cleanse my mind and body of thoughts, emotions and feelings and get them out into the open rather than bottling them up until they explode. And when

I'm reading, the feeling of being heard is intensified one hundred times or more because people are watching me, listening to me, hearing words I have created and formed into something meaningful, a poem. This is something I had only ever dreamt of before. I never thought I'd experience this feeling.

I have found I do have a talent. It may not be much in the greater scheme of things, but I do have a talent for writing and performing poetry and I've had people come up after a performance telling me how they enjoyed hearing me. This is a feeling that is almost indescribable, a feeling that you have given others pleasure through something you enjoy doing is amazing to experience.

I now look at the world in a whole new light. A tree is not just a tree anymore. What is it doing? How long has it been here? What has it seen? Does it have feelings and emotions like I do? I've discovered a whole new world out there thanks to writing and it's a world I lovingly embrace.

My writing has become a lot better too. I now put a lot more thought into what I write, how I write it and how I express myself through my writing. This has been reflected in my marks at university, which have improved a lot since I took up writing poetry. I write more concisely too and try not to waffle too much, which I did before.

My confidence has improved immensely as well. I have discovered that I can do things I only dreamt about before, that I do have a talent, that I do have a voice that people like and appreciate and that I can achieve a dream I previously thought impossible. This has led to a new-found self-belief in my abilities and in life too. I can do things that I never thought I could and, most importantly for me, I can give pleasure to others through my own writing creations.

And finally, and equally as important for me, I have found a whole new set of friends and a whole new community that appreciates me for being who I am, and who judge me on that and not on my Asperger's and how it affects me. This is quite possibly the greatest positive of all.

A Wooden War (by Andrew Smith)

remembering my father,
who would fashion a rifle
from an old block of wood
hand carved to
look like the Lee Enfield
he fought with in WWII
copper piping for a barrel
a nail for a trigger
that never moves
and off I would go
to fight in a war
where no-one got hurt
no-one got injured
no-one got killed and
we all returned with
limbs, eyes, brain intact
no need for crutches
as we ran through the
valleys and woods
that were our battlefields,
hiding behind bushes
climbing trees, leaping streams
jumping embankments before
we conquered the black hill
as we played out our war
with weapons of wood
the only scars we gathered
when we cut our knees and palms
as we ducked make believe bullets
that never hit our young bodies
and swore blind we had never been hit

how brave we felt playing our
pretend wars with weapons of wood
that never hurt anyone
and now I look back
and think how all wars should be fought this
    way
until exhausted from a day's playing and
    running
you go home for tea and a good night's sleep
and prepare to fight another day
in the only war our young minds understood
and our only fear was the telling off from our
mothers if we were late home

Chapter 7

Lifelines

*How I Manage My Autism to
Create a Positive Life Experience*

Tracy Turner

Introduction by Luke Beardon

Tracy's chapter reads to me as if it is very much centred around the concept of acceptance. As with others writing in this book, to be accepted for who one is can be essential to positive experiences. I fully believe that if a child (or adult) feels more comfortable engaging in a solitary activity (such as reading) and that reading is rewarding, as opposed to more 'traditional' children's activities (such as playing with others), then the child should be allowed and encouraged to read. After all, what suits one child will not suit another. I understand that relationships with others are very important, but more important in my opinion is the individual's mental health and levels of contentment. Rio clearly accepts Tracy for who she is, which is perhaps one of the reasons why she has such a good relationship with him. I think there is a lot to learn from this; learning from the individual about likes and dislikes seems pretty obvious – and yet so many people on the spectrum appear to have other people's likes and dislikes imposed upon them. Reading Tracy's chapter, it is abundantly clear that she gets a great deal of satisfaction from activities that don't involve other people, while at the same time having a deep connection with family members who accept her for being herself. It seems so obvious that accepting someone for who they are would be hugely important for anyone, but how many people with Asperger's syndrome (AS) are afforded that consideration?

I think 'bittersweet' describes life for everyone with its many ups and downs. I sometimes feel my life has been more bitter than sweet, but am trying to change my often negative mindset.

I am definitely liable to look on the darker side rather than the brighter side of life. I also tend to expect the worst in any given situation. I think this is so I can prepare myself: lots of 'bad' stuff has happened in my life – family bereavements especially – which I have struggled to deal with. I also suffer with the dreaded depression that seems to follow some of us 'Aspies' around like a dark cloud, ready to spring forth with a rain shower or downpour at the least expected moment. I tend to be either very up or very down. I don't appear to have much of an emotional range in between. I tend to think this is a very autistic way to be. Although a personal opinion (not a proven scientific fact), I have noticed that autistic people do not have a full range of emotions as others might express it, but very much 'extremes' of emotions, I notice this in myself and in my nephew, who is also diagnosed.

However, this chapter is about 'positive experiences' so I am going to focus on what is positive in my life. This will obviously also discuss those things that cause me some difficulty, as it is those things that push me and motivate me to find things that work for me and create feelings of calm within my soul (which is what I seek over feelings of happiness, which I rarely seem to attain). Do not let this sway you into thinking we are a negative bunch. I would not say this is true. I have, however, heard people comment that the reason we can appear younger than others is that our faces do not show a great deal of expression – smiles, frowns and so on – therefore, we do not wrinkle so easily! A blessing indeed.

Let me first give you some background. I was not diagnosed with Asperger's until I was 41. I was the typical misdiagnosed female throughout my 20s and 30s: always told I had depression, which I always asserted wasn't the true problem. Thus, I have spent most of my life so far feeling like I don't fit in, not knowing how to interact, being unable to express properly my thoughts and feelings, being 'different'; no wonder then that I was depressed! My nephew, diagnosed aged nine, will at least get the help and support he needs at a younger age, and have family around him who can build up his self-esteem and a knowledge that 'different' is okay. I, on the other hand, had to develop my own range of strategies to deal with this world I struggle in and don't always understand. These turned out to be my 'positive experiences' and I would always encourage others to find those things which make your soul happy, which make your heart sing and which just feel comfortable and right for you.

As a child my strategy was always and without ex-ception 'to withdraw'. I would take myself away from any circumstance or situation I found too challenging or uncomfortable, whether related to the environment, the people or just not knowing what was expected. This was, and probably still is, my most effective coping strategy. Although now I'm an adult I also have the option sometimes of not putting myself in that situation in the first place.

I found my solace in books mostly. Being able to read from a very young age, I would often be found immersed in a book or maybe writing something. I remember little about my childhood, I think I must have blocked a lot out. I do, however, remember clearly whenever we went anywhere I always had a bag with me. This contained activities I could do that didn't involve me engaging with anyone else – colouring books, drawing, reading books and probably a soft toy too. We would often go to friends of my mum's and all the kids would go off upstairs to play and I would stay sitting downstairs with my bag of activities in the room with the grown ups. I don't remember anything they spoke about, I was too busy in my own little world. I wouldn't talk to anyone and definitely didn't want anyone to talk to me. I can remember at home going and sitting under the stairs and reading the two big encyclopedias we kept on a shelf there. I still have a great thirst for knowledge and have always loved to read non-fiction, particularly books about nature, places and history. It is my way of making sense of the world around me. As a teenager I always wrote a diary, as it helped me to write about things that I didn't feel able to talk about. I still like to write about how I feel; this is often in poetry. This is a poem I wrote to try to encourage myself in a down period: I have times when I feel I can do nothing right, and I have to remind myself that I'm okay as I am and I don't need to change and be someone I am not.

Choose Life

We don't choose to live,
We can choose to make a difference.
Be bold, then be bolder still,
Aim high, put no ceiling on your dreams.
The sky is free, no obstruction here
On the ground barricades wherever you turn.
So look up, be inspired
Encourage others, encourage yourself,
Let your thoughts run wild
Your creativity spill over,
Put no constraints on your potential
Others will try to, don't let them.

You are you, they are they.
No-one can touch you
Be in tune with your Spirit
Your heart and your soul;
Only there will you find it
Fulfilment, satisfaction and peace
Be true to you
Wholly, completely,
Be free.

This is a much more natural way for me to communicate than talking. Sometimes the words just flood out of me like a running stream, almost with no beginning and no ending. It helps me to clear my head when I cannot rid it of the many, many thoughts that race around it each day (and night). I agree with Byron, the celebrated poet, as he says in his often-used quote, 'If I don't write to empty my mind, I go mad' (Lord George Gordon Byron, 1788–1824).

This is how I feel too. No-one would listen to all the stuff I have in my head, but it's important to me. In order to try and make some sense of myself I must write. Many an Aspie will tell you I'm sure, our brains are always on the go; it's like being on a permanent treadmill, exhausting, but I also feel blessed to have such a thoughtful and creative mind.

As well as poems I have started to write the words for worship songs, ever hopeful that one day somebody will put them to music. A lady at church has set two to music for me, and if I do say so myself, they sound pretty good. Hopefully, one day, other people will hear them and sing them too.

At school, although I will always say I hated school, it was learning that was a positive experience for me. I loved to learn, and it was the one thing I was good at. I could never (can never) remember anything I was told. Everything had to be written down. When revising for exams I would write out whole books. I was bright, but learning was hard work for me. My memory is not great, and I had to write things down over and over again to have any hope of remembering them. But, here at least, I could succeed. I remember how proud my mum and dad were in my first year of secondary school when I came top in all ten exams of different subjects. At last I could do something right. This made me work even harder. As I didn't really socialise or have friends, all I did was study and read. Therefore, this became a means of self-fulfilment, and I still love to learn new things.

Another of the things that has been really positive for me is owning a dog. My dog is called Rio and he is now 12 years old. I have always loved animals and I think they understand me better than most people. As a child growing up we had a lovely cat who could always be relied upon to give a good cuddle when needed. In keeping with the Asperger's traits, I have many sensory issues and one of these is touch. I am very funny about people touching me. If I'm upset, the last thing I want is someone to hug me, but an animal touch is so different. My dog has been really great and helped me through some very bad times. He is so loving and so non-judgemental. He is always up for a walk or a hug. He is so soft and adorable. Although we never had a dog when I was a child, both my aunts and uncles did. This again became a form of escape and coping for me. If we were round at a family gathering, I would always go off and walk the dog. I couldn't cope with people trying to talk to me, or looking at me even, but a dog was good company. I could go out, clear my head, enjoy the park and have a lovely dog with me too. Bliss. I often wonder, looking back, what my family thought of me. Did they think me anti-social or shy, unfriendly or weird? My parents and grandparents are dead now, so I cannot ask them. However, I will always be grateful and thankful that they let me be 'me'. They didn't, to my knowledge, try to make me do things I didn't want to do, or make me into someone I am not. They accepted me, eccentricity and all, and just loved me as I was. I am very much like my dad, so I assume they just thought I took after him, and that was that. I think that probably played a crucial role in me not falling so low in depression and self-worth, as I might otherwise have done.

I have moved a little off the point there. To return to my dog: I got him aged 14 weeks from a rescue centre. Since my mum had died suddenly I had really been struggling. I wasn't sleeping and would often walk my neighbour's dog and go for miles and miles. This was the only time that anything seemed to be right with my world. After about two years I decided to get my own dog. My sister was soon to move out and I didn't want to live alone. Although, often preferring my own company, I did, and still do, get lonely. I had intended to get a slightly older dog, not a puppy. However, at the rescue centre they all have their labels up – this one couldn't go with kids, that one couldn't go with cats, etc. I found a one-year-old that I really liked but upon enquiring was told he had been reserved earlier that day and they just hadn't changed the label. I was really upset and didn't go back for a while. Then my sister and I were driving back from somewhere completely unrelated one Sunday and we happened to drive past. She said, 'Let's just pop in', which we duly did, and there they were! Six abandoned puppies, all black and white, all adorable, eyes to melt the hardest heart. That was that. They had been put out that morning and there was one left. That was fate, he became my baby! I couldn't take him home straight away as he had ear infections, but I visited him after work every day. I took him for walks, taught him to sit and finally brought him home. He was, and still is, a delight. Everyone loves him; he's so placid and soppy. He goes practically everywhere with me and he's such a good boy. I have no children but he is my pride and joy (along with my nephew and niece of course). I love him to bits, and more importantly he loves me, just as I am.

That leads me on to one of my other great loves – nature. I am most at home and happiest when outside. So walking Rio is one of my favourite times of day. Whether it's hot or cold, wet or dry, we are out in the parks, the woods and the fields. I love to watch the changing seasons, to hear the birds in the trees, and to see the amazing sunrises and sunsets. It's as if there is no-one else in the world, just me, and Rio, God and his creations. These are the things that make my heart smile. I have seen some amazing sights – wild deer just popping in and out of the undergrowth, red kites flying overhead, seedlings taking root and the changing landscapes. My local park does nature walks so I have tracked bats, been on bird walks, caught and observed butterflies and damsel- and dragonflies. I love to see all the many species we are blessed to have in our countryside. They are all amazing. It enables me to find a 'calm' that I seldom attain indoors or in 'society'. It is quiet, peaceful and in harmony. It is one of the things that brings me great joy. There is nothing like a walk on a calm day, under a clear blue sky, with trees in blossom or leaf, breathing in the air and looking around at the sights. Beautiful!

The other place I most love to be is beside the sea. I love the beaches in this country: the scenery, the sandy or stony beach and the huge expanse of sea. I love to go on holiday or just to the coast for a day, usually to two or three favoured places on the south or east coast. I love to walk the cliffs of the South Downs and see the rivers join the sea. I like the freedom and the space and the fresh sea air. I always feel calm by the sea. It reminds me how small I am and how vast Earth is. The sea just stretches on for miles and miles. How great to live on an island, a rather big island, but surrounded by sea anyway. Being outside is so natural to me. Everything else brings disruption, noise, crowds, anxiety, expectation and feelings of inadequacy, not fitting in and being different.

The other great experience in my life is my family. I suppose because they know me so well, and I know them so well, it is a safe place to be. I can be myself, truly and completely. No pretending to be something I am not, no feelings of fear or distress. It is truly like coming home.

As a child I spent a lot of time with my nan and grandad, my mum's parents. They truly devoted a lot of time to us, especially after my parents divorced when I was seven. As a very small child I would hide from them in a corner, not wanting to look at them, or them at me. I was too shy to talk to them. But gradually their love for me won through, and next to home it became my favourite place to be. Here I was at home; I was loved. I could be myself. I would often walk around the corner to their house. I remember my nan patiently teaching me to knit when I was about five. I would watch her and learnt to cook Sunday dinner, wash by hand, garden. My grandad taught me to dust and keep house (he was a modern man even in those days!), to decorate and do simple jobs around the house. All have been invaluable to me in living an independent life. I owe them such a lot. They were always patient, always kind. We would sit at their breakfast table and watch the birds in their garden, looking them up in their bird book. It was from them I learnt to love nature and care for it. As they got older I would go round and help them with little tasks, shopping and changing the beds. Whilst other teenagers were out with their mates, I was with my grandparents, loved and accepted; again, allowed to be 'me'.

More recently, my sister and her kids have been the light of my life. I love to spend time with them. I share my love of outside with the kids, going to the parks, climbing trees, paddling in the river, going on a bug hunt. My nephew is very much like me. We have always got on so well. They enrich my life in so many ways. They are full of energy and enthusiasm, which makes me smile (I feel not much else makes me smile, I am a rather serious person on the whole). I am so blessed to have them in my life. I love being an auntie. It is such a privilege to have a role in their lives. I hope I can be a good role model to them and they can learn what it is to accept and love yourself for who you are, rather than feel judged by the views of others.

Finally, I want to share with you my faith. I am a Christian, and my belief in God is so strong and present in my life. I love that God made me 'just as I am' and God doesn't make mistakes. I don't really question why I am like this; I just accept it is me. Everyone has faults and positives, strengths and weaknesses and I am no different. God blessed me with an intelligent mind, a creative ability and a caring heart, and for this I am grateful. I love to go to church and sing praises to the One who is greater than all others. I like being part of something bigger than myself. Church has its own challenges. It is another place where I often feel on the periphery, a little like an outsider looking in. Although people are friendly, I can't say I have really made friends there. Not people to meet out of church or do things with. Some of the groups are a bit 'cliquey'. I find that a challenge. But I do feel comfortable and want to keep going and that is the most important thing.

I know faith is not for everyone, and I respect that. But, for me, it is like an anchor on a stormy sea. It gives me a way of grounding myself. Even when things go wrong, I know I can submit to a greater, higher power. God is in control and I can turn it over to Him and let Him take care of it. This has been hard to learn and it doesn't exactly come easily to me, but I'm getting there. I believe I am a work in progress, and He is growing me into the person He wants me to be, for His purposes and for the glory of God.

So this is a summary of all that is positive in my life and the things that sustain me. Daily life, work in particular, shopping, noise, people in general are a struggle for me. I face challenges each and every day, but I am able to focus on these things which are good for me. These positive experiences help me to make my way through life; to live not just to endure. They help me to focus and to live a fulfilling, not merely a frustrating, life. They remind me of the good and happy times and this helps me to counterbalance the inevitable challenges that come my way. Writing them down has really helped me to identify what works well for me (it's easy for me to know the things to avoid!). I think it will be easier to try and do more of the good stuff. I hope that everyone reading this will be able to identify that which is good and valuable in their own lives, and to make the most of that. I always try to remember 'we only get one shot at it' – we need to do the best we can, with what we've got, while we are able to. Very philosophical eh? So these are my positive experiences; I hope you can find yours.

Chapter 8

Positive Experiences of Being on the Autistic Spectrum
Personal Reflections from Joanna Treasure

Joanna Treasure

Introduction by Luke Beardon

This is a truly inspirational chapter that is superbly well written with intelligence and honesty. Joanna's perspectives on aspects such as diagnosis (why does one need to be 'problematised' before getting a diagnosis?) are brilliantly presented and well worth a great deal of rumination. It is refreshing indeed to read a line such as 'Speaking personally, looking back at the most successful and enjoyable aspects of my life, I feel that I must attribute all of them to my autistic personality.'

Joanna makes some excellent points, not least her thoughts on 'severity' and 'mild', which are thought-provoking and persuading. She also makes some profound observations on the concept of a spectrum, as well as the issues around differing views of autism and how difficult it is when there is a lack of consensus around what people are actually observing when interacting with autistic people. I won't go on summarising Joanna's work – she does a far better job of it than I ever could. I will, however, just note the point Joanna makes about having 'passionate interests' – though within certain diagnostic manuals this might read 'obsessions'; in the *Diagnostic and Statistical Manual of Mental Disorders, 5th edition (DSM-5)* within the diagnostic criteria for 'autism spectrum disorder' 3B states: 'Highly restricted, fixated interests that are abnormal in intensity or focus (e.g. strong attachment to or preoccupation with unusual objects, excessively circumscribed or perseverative interest).' Joanna does a beautiful job of demonstrating that what can be seen by some as a 'disorder', within other contexts can be seen as an absolute positive.

Three years ago, at the age of 50, I discovered that I am autistic, living my life as a hitherto unidentified example of Asperger's syndrome. This was a bit unexpected, as I had previously thought that I had a good understanding of autism and the various ways in which it is generally known to present. In another way, it was no surprise at all as I had already suspected it in myself although I had not managed to match up my personality against the usual 'thumbnail sketch' descriptions.

In retrospect, the main reason for my previous failure to identify Asperger's in myself is that, since infancy, I had learnt to conceal and even suppress some of the features by which Asperger's may become recognised, and had been so successful in compensating for the well-described social and communication difficulties that I have been able to pass as normal, as if I were a neurotypical person, albeit one with recurrent difficulties that have kept cropping up throughout my life.

Thanks to the work of Judith Gould and Jacqueline Ashton-Smith, it is gradually becoming better recognised that this potential to go below the radar, living with Asperger's and any associated issues as a hidden disability, is associated with the feminine pattern of presentation – which is more often seen in females although it also occurs in a proportion of males – and is a frequent cause of missed diagnosis or misdiagnosis.[1] If we are highly motivated to fit into social groups and have the capacity to be both observant and also able to manage and control our behaviour sufficiently well, we can learn to copy conventional styles of interacting – but the effort of keeping up the performance is exhausting and stressful. So much depends on the circumstances we find ourselves in: if those around us are insensitive or unkind, they may tease or criticise, which only adds to the stress, but if people around us are secure enough to be able to accommodate others just as they are, life can go sweetly with no significant problems arising.

Within a few months, I had researched the subject with my usual focus, creativity, attention to detail and tendency to perseveration...and by the time I'd read several blogs and books by female Aspies in particular, I had come to realise that their personal accounts corresponded so well with my own that I knew that my identification as an Aspie was entirely accurate.

I also noticed that I now felt more integrated as a human being than I had since the age of ten.

I welcomed my diagnosis with a genuine sense of celebration. This was partly because it has been so enlightening in helping me to understand myself so much better than before, explaining my recurrent experiences of not easily fitting in within predominantly neurotypical social settings. More importantly, I welcome my Asperger's personality as I recognise that it accounts for many of the most positive aspects of my life too.

---

1   Gould, J. (2011) 'Missed diagnosis or misdiagnosis? Girls and women in the autism spectrum.' The NAS Lorna Wing Centre for Autism. Available at www.slideshare.net/NationalAutisticSociety/plenary-session-1-judith-gould), accessed 23 October 2016.

So, I need to introduce myself. In the spirit of the overarching theme of this book, I have chosen to highlight what I regard as the most positive aspects of my multifaceted personality. This has forced me to resist my deeply ingrained and realistic modesty in order to present the things about myself that I most value for the way in which they enhance and enrich my experience of life – so please understand the following paragraphs in this light, by way of a meditation on self-appreciation.

I am Jo – and I am autistic. I have been blessed with good fortune enough to become a loved wife and a mother. I am a musician (listener, singer, composer and arranger, modest pianist, occasional horn player and fond jazzer), a nature lover (stargazer, looker at wild flowers and trees, bird lover and pond peerer), an enthusiast for the visual arts, an occasional designer (including two large pieces of highly personalised oak storage furniture but more often of my children's cake decorations or roughly made dress-up gear), a sportswoman (having rowed for two of my universities and now enjoying orienteering at a modest improver's level) and a very happy dancer (both for fitness and for sheer pleasure). I am also an academic and evidence-based scientist, having trained as a doctor and worked for 20 years in NHS hospitals, pursing a career as a histocytopathologist, including nine years at consultant level. I am an educationalist and a workshop facilitator. I am a keen observer, reflective thinker, truth seeker and communicator, fond of languages and role play. I enjoy comedy of many sorts – including a willingness to find entertainment in my own idiosyncrasies.

I am a counsellor and advocate – first and foremost for my own vulnerable self, naturally for my children but also for others if and when there is an opportunity to contribute something of use if only by way of moral support for their cause (which I count as a great privilege as it adds a fulfilling and meaningful quality to my day). When I have had problems, I have endeavoured to learn from them. My insights have been valuable in both private and professional contexts. Positive experiences of deriving support and long-term benefit from several humanistic counselling relationships over the decades led me to studying the subject at adult evening classes (counselling certification at levels 2 and 3). In parallel, I have found cognitive therapy extremely good – I trained myself from 1988 onwards from David Burns' 1980 book, *Feeling Good – The New Mood Therapy* (Harper).

Since being fortunate enough to be introduced to Solution Focused Brief Therapy by Vicky Bliss, following my diagnosis, and having studied her book in detail with my usual thoroughness (E. Veronica Bliss and Genevieve Edmonds, *A Self-Determined Future with Asperger Syndrome: Solution Focused Approaches*, Jessica Kingsley Publishers, 2007), I have found this approach to be so remarkably beneficial to me that I now regularly keep the principles in mind and continue to notice the positive benefits of doing so.

Reflecting on positive aspects of my autistic personality

The first thing that sings out from that list is the fact that I engage in passionate interests!

Whatever activity has my attention, I tend to engage in it with full attention, so as to get the most out of it that I can. I am capable of intense focus, dedication and perseverance when things get tough. My medical career was extremely demanding and challenging but I know I always did my best, with honest commitment, effort and great attention to detail. I particularly enjoyed all of the teaching opportunities that came my way. I think this is because learning gives me great personal satisfaction – and it is delightful to help others to learn and to share in and witness how good they can feel about their own learning progress.

I am highly attuned to pattern and structure. This is apparent in my scientific pursuits but it is also extremely relevant to my musical appreciation and creativity. I grew up surrounded by all sorts of music – I was hearing it, remembering it, analysing it even from the cradle, and writing it by the time I reached my early teens. If my medical career had not taken precedence, I like to think that I might have achieved more in my compositional development overall, and yet I cannot deny the pleasure I feel at having produced certain favourite pieces, even if there may be few others who would share as much enthusiasm over them as I do.

Perhaps even more important to me than composing is that I have greatly valued all of the opportunities I have had to make music happen live, sharing with other like-minded people in the creative process in real time, especially in front of an attentive audience, which produces such an intense atmosphere. The act of performance is scary at times but it is also an exhilaration to be transported in the moment during that shared experience of musical creation, for the sole purpose of conveying that piece of music to whoever is in that moment wanting to pay attention to it.

I am highly systematic in my approach to sorting and organising information. This has clearly been beneficial for research, academic study and carrying out my professional roles to a high standard.

My appreciation of logic and order enables me to respect well-considered protocols and sound evidence-based practice. There are also useful benefits to any kind of research in the home setting, whether you are checking out the 'best buys' against your own checklist of desired specifications before acquiring white goods or planning travel arrangements for a holiday.

All these are particularly useful attributes.

They are also features and characteristics which are often associated with autistic personalities.

They are found embedded in all of the best descriptions of autistic people – but they are not always highlighted, simply because they are not actually 'problems'.

Conventional descriptions of autism in adults on websites such as NHS choices and that of the National Autistic Society generally describe the so-called 'triad' of impairments – having difficulties in the areas of social communication, social interaction and social imagination, although it's worth pointing out that Francesca Happé has advised caution against assuming more than a coincidence of occurrence in these three types of difficulties, in articles such as 'Time to give up on a single explanation for autism'.[2]

Those of us who have such social difficulties may indeed experience confusion over sarcasm or figures of speech, and may be inclined to take other people's speech more literally than intended. We may find it tricky to gauge the appropriate level of formality or familiarity to adopt under varying circumstances and we may find greetings and goodbyes awkward to navigate. Even if we don't feel a need to keep to familiar routines in order to feel secure, we may prefer to have more information available in order to maintain a sense of control, so as to make informed choices from alternative options, and to have extra time allowed us to process what is being communicated to us. However, provided such preferences are accepted and accommodated, they needn't cause much inconvenience to others. As long as there is a reasonable amount of tolerance of everyone's preferences, with a decent measure of acceptance of difference, there need be no problem. Real social difficulties may only arise for us when we are put under excessive pressure to conform in ways that don't come naturally, especially if we are then

2   Happé, F., Ronald, A. and Plomin, R. (2006) 'Time to give up on a single explanation for autism.' *Nature Neuroscience 9*, 10, 1218–1220. Available at http://dept.wofford.edu/neuroscience/NeuroSeminar/pdfFall2011/4-explaining-autism.pdf, accessed 23 October 2016.

teased, bullied or ostracised for struggling. Unfortunately, the adverse effects of such experiences can be cumulative.

However, under circumstances in which clear, concise and accurate patterns of communication are valued we may not be at any disadvantage at all. Social chit chat may not be our best strength, but there are contexts in which it can be far more useful to have people present who are good at being precise and straightforward, keeping to the point, willing to persevere, passionate in pursuing their interests and able to be systematic and logical in their approach to their work.

Autistic – alien or human?

So, I am on the autistic spectrum and I celebrate that. I'm still on the human spectrum too though, and that feels important to me. We need to ensure that autistic individuals are not missing out on the full entitlement associated with our rightful place as human citizens during repeated references to being 'on the spectrum', as that can almost begin to sound as if it is intended to imply something more 'other' than properly human.

Many autistic authors and bloggers do actually describe themselves as feeling like alien beings.

Asperger's people who use this analogy in their written accounts are doing so consciously – there is no suggestion that they are actually questioning whether they may truly have been translocated through space and time in some physical or supernatural sense. (Those individuals who might espouse such a notion too strongly would probably already be on drugs for presumed psychotic delusional illness rather than being supported to describe and communicate their feelings to others.)

So, despite the potential risks involved in expressing unconventional ideas and perceptions, it is readily apparent that autistic adults who have the capacity both to reflect on their experiences and to communicate their thoughts with others quite often describe it as feeling like an alien being. They describe their growing awareness of feeling so 'other', and of being so unable to fit in naturally into their immediate social environment, that it seems as if they might as well be aliens who have discovered themselves to be growing up in a world that is clearly foreign to them, such that they cannot perceive it as being a correct match for them, as if they recognised that they were never going to identify with this Earth, this human society, as a true home. A well-established internet Asperger's forum has embraced this analogy by adopting it in its name of 'Wrong Planet'. I hasten to point out that other well-established forum sites are available. The UK-based aspievillage.co.uk forum, for example, has adopted an alternative perspective in its name, 'Aspie Village', representing a virtual community that is more Asperger's-friendly than the predominantly neurotypical society generally tends to be.

It never occurred to me to liken myself to an alien from another planet, but I think that was simply because I had identified plenty enough reasons to rationalise my 'differentness' from most of my peers so there was no need to refer to such an analogy. As I grew up, an introspective and reflective child and teenager, noticing that I felt different from the average child within the classroom or home neighbourhood, I attributed this to certain key factors in my upbringing, which appeared to explain it readily. This was in three main respects: I was (i) highly intelligent, (ii) highly musical and (iii) part of an unusually large family. These features were evident to me as I became conscious of them and came as a package – I happened to have been born into an unusually large family of highly intelligent siblings who had all been given individual private music lessons as well as taking part in four-part harmony singing around the piano and a wide range of other musical activities. Growing up surrounded by music-making since infancy, it felt as natural as a mother-tongue to a bilingual speaker.

My mother had high aspirations for her children to make the best use of all of the educational and other opportunities available. She was proud to see all of us graduate through university and onto various career pathways. There was also a great deal of other activity in the household, which I remember as being fun and exciting, including parties and visitors. (As far as my recollections of childhood will allow me to judge, I think that our lifestyle and habits may have been entirely typical of the wider community in other respects.)

If I tended to identify with people older than myself it was easy to attribute this to the fact that I happened to be the youngest, so most of the social life in the household involved the peer groups of my older siblings. When I noticed my difficulties in relating to children of my own age, I attributed that to lack of practice – since the house was so hectic, there wasn't much occasion for my parents to arrange playdates. In retrospect, this is more of a rationalisation to explain away my social awkwardness in a way that was considerate to myself and my circumstances, even if it was a mistaken view.

I was aware of being very 'bright' for my age as Mam celebrated the fact that I could read even before going to school – having been taught by an older sister. After only two terms in my first school, because I was complaining of boredom, Mam consulted an educational psychologist, who immediately organised a place for me at an independent private school on a full scholarship. (Later I discovered that my reading and comprehension skills scored so highly that my IQ was calculated to be equivalent to 170, no doubt an overestimate reflecting the coaching I'd received, but still definitely outside of the normal range.)

The effect of all this on my life was that I was uprooted from my socio-economic peer group in the first primary school where I'd just begun to settle down and maybe make a friend or two, and plonked down in a strange new world full of affluent kids who seemed to be far more confident than me – so now I had a readily apparent reason to explain away any further feelings of not fitting in with social groups. This feeling became only more intense when a blossoming of academic ability subsequently led me to one of the most elite girls' public schools (on a partial scholarship) then through Cambridge, Guy's and a 20-year career as a hospital doctor, mostly in pathology.

My passionate musical interests led me to live a kind of double life as I engaged in rather esoteric music-making interests including composing my own music, which was usually a very private activity apart from one week a year when I was able to mix with other composers at a summer school. That became a home from home, where I truly felt comfortable in my own skin, at least whilst actively engaged in workshops and concert performances if not always at other times.

Rainbow – a favourite analogy for 'the autistic spectrum'

The rainbow, and the wonderful array of its constituent colours, is symbolic of celebrating diversity in general. In particular, it has come to be closely associated with positive perspectives on autism, because of the range of difference encompassed within that one word. Indeed, some authors recommend that we refer to 'autisms' as a plural, since it is recognised that the characteristic features of autism can be identified within a range of developmental and syndromic contexts, all of which implies that a single source of causation would appear to be most unlikely.

So, the 'autistic rainbow' is a beautiful concept.

It very prettily illustrates the important fact that within autism (or, indeed, within 'the autisms'), there is a whole range of expression of whatever 'being autistic' may be. That's all good.

A question does arise for me, though, when people are described as being 'on the spectrum'. If we are being viewed as being 'on the autistic spectrum', where exactly are we being placed on the 'human spectrum'? Through the language of assigning autistic personalities so much to a position of 'otherness', there is a risk that we are being denied full identity as human beings.

Please don't misunderstand me though: I don't want to throw the (metaphorical) baby out with the bathwater – I love the colours of the rainbow and I fully appreciate the underlying spectral conceptualisation...but a spectrum is actually a very linear concept. The reality of human neurodiversity is far more multidimensional. Let's add some depth and profundity to enrich the concept, so as to enhance our true appreciation of the full range of qualities expressed within autistic people, just as within all human beings.

The main thing that autistic people have in common is that we share certain features that are generally identified as being shared by 'people with autism', and that we happen to share enough of them in order to 'qualify' for the diagnosis in the opinion of whichever diagnostician has been consulted. The over-riding quality of what we are understood to share is that we all tend to experience difficulties.

We wouldn't tend to find out about being autistic unless there were some difficulties causing us to present to some kind of clinician for a diagnostic assessment – but this leads to a mistaken presumption that being autistic is necessarily a bad thing! In a way, it is made out to be a bad thing by definition – because I suspect that clinicians would not be inclined to assign the diagnosis to anyone who should happen to score strongly on autistic screening charts *unless* they were also experiencing difficulties. I suspect they would either say that there was no need for a diagnosis, or that the diagnosis could not apply without the presence of difficulties.

This is the inevitable consequence of the problem-orientated approach to diagnosis, and it is understandable how it has arisen. If individuals are brought to the clinician's attention because of having problems, they need a diagnostic label to account for their problems in order that they may receive help. Conversely, if they don't seem to have problems requiring help, then they won't be given the diagnostic label.

We need help to resolve problems – but we don't necessarily need help just for showing autistic characteristics – and yet many of the so-called 'autistic characteristics' are described solely in negative ways rather than being acknowledged as potential positives. A more balanced view would be that the same features which are positive and beneficial when present within a balanced personality may prove to be troublesome in autism simply on account of being present in an extreme degree of expression or just through not being sufficiently balanced out by other characteristics – but that doesn't necessarily make them intrinsically bad features.

My feeling is that, in an ideal world, it could be envisaged as possible to identify how autistic any of us may actually be, without that being regarded as a negative thing. Help could still be directed towards a person only if and when help was required.

Exactly how autistic are we? The negative effect of denigratory language

Diagnosticians refer to certain severely disabled individuals as being 'severely autistic'.

I understand exactly what is meant by this and I would have had no qualms about using the same terminology myself in the past. After all, if individuals are unable to look after their own needs effectively, or even to communicate with others, they are certainly in need of support and care, so we understand them to be severely disabled in respect of their need to have others enable them to live well and safely. The severity of their disability is self-evident, but I am troubled at hearing the descriptor 'severe' being applied to autism, since I learnt to recognise myself as being autistic. Now, hearing that phrase troubles me because it implies a view that being autistic is intrinsically bad. In place of 'severely autistic' I would ideally prefer to hear 'extremely autistic' or, perhaps, 'severely disabled due to marked autism'.

Similarly, I don't find it helpful to describe Asperger's syndrome as 'mild autism'. Who is to judge exactly how autistic we are in comparison with those who are unable to communicate sufficiently well to complete the questionnaires?

Perhaps we may be very markedly autistic too, but the point is that if we also happen to have abilities to learn, to communicate, to express ourselves, to adapt to our circumstances and to behave in a way that enables us to fit into a role in society (to whatever extent that we manage it), these additional compensatory skills may be sufficient to enable autism to be entirely positive in its expression without any downsides. That scenario would surely explain some of our greatest idiosyncratic personalities – extreme creatives, innovative scientists, entrepreneurs and visionary leaders.

This means that some people who are regarded as great human beings are celebrated, praised and honoured exactly *because* they happen to have autistic characteristics in their make-up.

Autistic genes and natural selection – the sickle cell analogy

It would be unrealistic to suggest viewing all things autistic in an entirely positive light. The full range of the spectrum includes many individuals who are entirely dependent on others for support and care – and those of us with Asperger's syndrome are well aware of problems we experience. This leads many to ask why on Earth we should have these autistic genes persisting in our populations' gene pools? Why have they not disappeared through the process of natural selection?

I have some thoughts to offer on this, as I keep remembering something I learnt, as a medical student, about sickle cell disease. This is far more common in certain populations, including those originating in parts of the Mediterranean and parts of central Africa, and their diaspora wherever they now live.

Sickle cell anaemia is the full-blown version due to having a double dose of the faulty gene, which leads to 'sickling' of the red blood cells at low oxygen levels – causing very painful and life-threatening crises. Sickle cell trait is a much less problematic version of the disease resulting from having one faulty gene and one normal gene – so that only around half of the haemoglobin molecules have the fault and the cell sickling tendency is not so severe. So, why do some populations include so many individuals carrying this faulty gene that a significant number have the terrible suffering of the full-blown disease? Why doesn't natural selection stop it from happening?

It turns out that even though the double-dose version is terrible and often fatal, having the single-dose version is actually beneficial if you live in an area where malaria is endemic, because you are less likely to die from malaria!

Autism is way, way, *way* more complicated, probably involving many, *many* genes, it seems. But I think the principle may still apply: having autistic traits in the population is beneficial for humanity. Having too many of them, and/or, in more extreme versions – well that's still fine as long as you can flourish in your own way and be accepted – but the more different you are from typical people, the less likely you will be able to flourish and be accepted. It all depends on the overall mix of 'autistic' and other personality traits... And on the environment you happen to find yourself in... And on how much in the way of secondary problems you accumulate along the way, due to the trauma of repeated prejudice and misunderstanding, or even just due to the strain and stress of the constant effort you are making to overcome difficulties.

I used to ask myself, 'Why am I such a failure as a human being?', and I wasn't able to take pride in my talents and strengths because I was taught to view them as God-given talents which it was my responsibility to make the best use of.

Since I found out about my being autistic, it has helped me to turn my ideas around, to reframe the dysfunctional self-perceptions of being 'a failure', as I now realise that it is far more logical to realise that I do pretty well, all things considered.

Conclusions

Autistic characteristics are all useful qualities which are present in humans to varying extents.

All of the traits and features by which autism is identified in any individual's personality are valuable characteristics in themselves, and present in our gene pool because of their great importance to humanity. Consider how, in a well-balanced personality, having abilities to focus with close attention to detail, to stick faithfully to effective routines and protocols, to persevere in a single-minded manner without being easily distracted by inconsequential social interactions are really useful attributes and are worthy of celebration.

Of course, it all comes down to the overall balance: the results of the specific mix of genes present in the DNA code coupled with good fortune or otherwise in one's upbringing and circumstances. Whether any individual's personality turns out to be more robust or less, more capable or less, more suited to certain situations and roles than to others, independent or dependent on help and support, is down to the total effect of nature and nurture – exactly what combination of genes is inherited, how the embryo develops and what influences are present during the child's upbringing.

It does trouble me to note that when researchers report differences observed in autism, the language they use is so often overwhelmingly negative, even without yet fully understanding what they are observing or knowing its significance.

Speaking personally, looking back at the most successful and enjoyable aspects of my life, I feel that I must attribute all of them to my autistic personality. Discovering that Asperger's syndrome applies to me has shed new light on my recurrent difficulties, but it also accounts for so many of the successes and joys in my life, which have been realised through the intensity of my focus and the passion and perseverance with which I have engaged in various specific interests.

Continuing personal development has always been an important part of my life and this has involved plenty of evaluative reflection. Whenever I review various life experiences, one thing that has become very apparent to me is that the attitude of other people makes a huge difference. If people are insensitive, impatient and intolerant, my stress levels rise rapidly, and the difficulty of maintaining an illusion of composure becomes so much harder. Conversely, if people around me are open-minded and relaxed enough to give me enough breathing space to adjust to the situation, my life is so much easier and I am far more likely to be able to give of my best.

In a true spirit of valuing neurodiversity, I believe it is important to recognise and appreciate the positive qualities in all of us. The more we can accept and appreciate the full range of human potential, the better our lives can be. We all benefit from having autistic genes in our shared gene pool.

We must persuade society to value all of these positive aspects of autism.

Only by doing that can we begin to understand how humankind is so much the stronger for being neurodiverse.

Chapter 9

A Year in Normandy

*Learning a Foreign
Language and Culture*

Dean Worton

Introduction by Luke Beardon

I have known Dean for several years and love reading his writing. He's one of those people who just makes so much sense! What pervades throughout Dean's chapter for me is not one specific thing that is inherently positive, but the underlying theme of Dean as a positive person himself. His philosophy appears to be that optimism promotes positive outcomes, and to accept that things won't always go to plan but to recognise that the individual does have a certain amount of control is a positive stance. Having a focus on something that can have the potential to make one happy and to proactively engage with it sounds simple, but, as people who have suffered from depression will tell you, it most certainly is not that easy. Dean is a fantastic example of someone who ensures that he has enough positive activities in his daily routine to engage in, with the aim of reducing the risk of feeling down. His optimism and outlook on life are an inspiration to me, and I believe his inner strength is to be greatly admired.

How it all began

In 1999 I obtained a degree in languages and business from Leeds Metropolitan University in Leeds, England. As an Aspie, i.e. a person with Asperger's syndrome (AS), this could sound incredibly daunting, because, as well as having to study in England for three years, I also had to do a year of study abroad. I don't remember feeling nervous about this, however, it wasn't all plain sailing.

The timing was very apt as the death of Princess Diana took place in France the day before I set off for the same country. The storyline of the French film *Amélie* (Jean-Pierre Jeunet, 2001), which happens to be my favourite film, was about what happened after Amélie heard this shock news, and decided to live her life to the full, which is just what I did for the next year. Whether intentional or not, the character displays several characteristics of Asperger's syndrome, and I'm sure that many Aspies who have seen the film will be able to relate to Amélie's ways. Both adventures began in the same week, although unlike *Amélie*, which was a work of fiction, my adventure was real.

My first day

I arrived at the halls of residence in Le Havre, Normandy, France at 9.00 am on Tuesday 2 September 1997. Once shown to my room and shown by the landlady how everything worked, I was left to my own devices for the next 24 hours. Although I knew the address of the college, I didn't know exactly where that was. All was not lost as I had been encouraged to seek out the two Irish girls who were to become my best friends for the next year. I was told to wait until the afternoon. This was fine as I needed rest. As an Aspie, though, imagine yourself in this situation. Here I was abroad and knew nobody but the head of business studies, who drove me from the port, and the stern-looking landlady. Would you have the courage to knock on their door? I did feel very apprehensive, and part of me thought about not being there to meet English-speaking people, but after thinking it all through, I knew how odd it would be not to seek out their company. It would have been harder to do if I had not been told that they were looking forward to meeting me, but I'm much better able to make approaches towards strangers where they are already expecting me. It's when it is unexpected that I can procrastinate for days and even months, and lose opportunities.

Group One

As there were 140 students in the year, there were five 'main' groups. The seven English speakers (Anglophones) were split between four of the groups and put into three pairs plus one person on their own. I was the person placed in a group with no other Anglophones, Group One. It's a foregone conclusion that the other Anglophones all sat together in their pairs talking to one another in English; so I felt lucky as I was there to be around French speakers and only French speakers, although, as the token Aspie of the Anglophones, this was a huge challenge because I had to use all of my inner resources. I did not have access to the metaphorical key that helps people to interact with people who they are not used to with ease. People have always thought that this is due to being socially phobic; however, I can actually be very social and feel confident even with strangers, but my mind needs to understand what is going on first and my response time is too slow. As a result, I can be a seemingly very silent person, who looks like he either dislikes everyone in his environment or is absolutely terrified of them. Actually, I'm able to interact very well and be a good conversationalist when the right conditions are met and I have some control over my environment.

Whilst I did have a small amount of contact with some of my classmates in Group One and a few conversations initiated by classmates (most of whom were female and probably trying to include me), none of them actually became my friend. As a result, I spent most classes sitting alone, or next to someone random who didn't necessarily even say hello to me. Fortunately at that point we were only three months away from the last class as we only did classes for just over six months. Other people in this position would be very upset, but I possess the Aspie ability of separating logic from emotion and also being patient and resilient and liking to look at the positives. I was learning a new language and discovering a whole new different teaching style. I've always enjoyed learning about different cultures, and I've always thought that learning anything about France is intriguing. Being the token foreigner in Group One and silently observing really was like being a fly on the wall.

The timetable

I had a rather peculiar timetable by comparison to what I was used to. The hours were even longer than they had been back at school, amounting to 32 hours per week. We were studying towards a 'Diplome Universtaire de Technologie (DuT)', best translated as university business diploma, which was equal to two-thirds of a standard degree.

Monday mornings were devoted purely to examinations, often starting at 8.00 am with a 90-minute lesson in the afternoon. I had an hour on Tuesday mornings at 9.00 am and then some lessons in the afternoon. Wednesdays started at 8.00 am and lasted until 7.00 pm with very few breaks. On Thursday, there was an hour-long law lecture at 8.00 am with Enterprise Group in the morning and French in the afternoon. The latter two classes were the two most easy-going items on my timetable. Fridays lasted from 9.00 am until 6.30 pm and I was even in class from 10.30 am until noon on Saturdays. Subjects included high-level mathematics, accounting, law, computing, French and various business modules. Some subjects were difficult and/ or boring. There were others that I really enjoyed.

One thing I especially liked was learning German taught in French. It was a bizarre experience, yet somehow felt easy and natural. Maybe only an Aspie could adapt easily to this. I almost passed the course but not quite as it's a difficult course for anyone from abroad. However, I'm very proud of my efforts and it was a very rich experience. Enterprise Group was interesting as there were about a dozen Enterprises run by the students themselves based on various topics. Mine was based on international trade and my role was simply to promote my home university and the good things about the UK.

Routines

One thing that is common amongst Aspies is having a routine. I've never been someone who has to do the same thing at the same time every day, but that are certain things that I try to fit in to each day, and feel uncomfortable when they are missing. They are mostly centred around diet and exercise. If I'm able to keep to these habits, I'm usually quite happy. The main one is walking for at least 30 minutes a day. It doesn't have to be a set route and I much prefer going somewhere slightly different each time. I feel happiest when I end up somewhere new because I love exploring and what could be more thrilling than exploring a city abroad? As this is not something that most other people are bothered about, I usually did this on my own, and greatly enjoyed this because I could be alone with my thoughts in silence. If I had the chance I would go out for a walk in my lunch-break and this would help me to get through a difficult and stressful day at college.

On Sunday nights, I usually only had five hours of sleep due to exam revision. This resulted in having to grab sleep whenever I could in the early part of the week. Many people don't need to catch up with lost sleep and I wish I were one of them but I'm not. It was futile trying to go to bed earlier because there was so much chatting going on in the rooms nearby, which simply made it impossible. It was easier to simply go round and join in as I was going to be listening to it either way. This meant that on some of the other nights, I was in bed below my minimum level of eight hours. I had no option but to take naps during specific free periods as it was the only way that I could stay awake for the classes. Aspies are not always keen if things are not on their own terms, but equally some Aspies, myself included, have a very stoical nature. I simply made a routine from all of this, but these were moments alone, and sometimes having naps at times when you don't expect to be disturbed can be quite nice. Due to it being the only time available to do so, just before 9.00 am every Tuesday, I bought two laundry tokens, took my clothes to get washed, went for my one class of the morning, returned, transferred the clothes into the dryer, went for a nice nap, went back down at a specific time, brought the clothes back to my room, hung them up and soon afterwards went back to college again to have lunch. As strange as it sounds, all these routines brought me comfort.

Food consumption

All of the Anglophones had to rely on the college canteen for lunch during the week. There were set dishes each day and we had very little choice. Snails and frogs legs were never on the menu, and I have never seen these items, but more than once I ate tongue. The canteen was the place where I was most likely to be approached by the French students in the group, and sometimes if I was alone, they would sit with me. All we had in the halls was a portable stove each, and one fridge between all seven of us. Two actually, but one broke down quickly! The local supermarket sold freezer bags, and some of us including myself used to attach these bags to the inside handles of our windows and leave them hanging on the outside of the windows. It did look a bit odd from the street nearby, but it went unmentioned and unchallenged for a whole year and it worked. It kept the weekend food fresh overnight and we could eat it!

Doing things my own way can also make me feel happier, sometimes even when the idea is quirky. Even though I cannot take credit for the idea of hanging a bag outside my window, it is another Aspie trait to think outside the box. Sometimes Aspies do things that might be considered odd to the outside world, but generally if it is doing no harm to yourself or others (and provided that it is not going to cause bullying beyond one or two throw-away comments that could be ignored), then I think sometimes it could be worth carrying out whatever unusual act it is. Very often the so-called odd ideas are the best ones, and many things that today the world takes for granted were once considered ridiculous. So if ever you have an idea that you and everyone else thinks seems ridiculous, it might just be a future invention that will change the world.

Work placement

We also had to carry out ten weeks of work experience. Unfortunately, I was asked to leave my placement after just four weeks due to 'allegations' of not communicating despite thinking that I did! I never did find out in exactly what way I was thought to not communicate. It could be something as simple as walking into an office and not shaking each person's hand, but when you're in a country that does things a different way, sometimes there might be no point in trying to understand. This was unpleasant, disheartening and created the awkward situation of having to do the last few weeks at the college with my course leader's office being my base. However, although it ended badly and the organisation should have handled it better than they did, I'm not going to base my judgement of that organisation and all French employers solely on what happened to me. I've also had bad experiences in British workplaces for similar reasons. I still want to look at the positive side of having worked there at all. At least, I have experienced working in a French organisation, in this case the local social housing offices, and it was interesting to see the work that was going on, and to have the opportunity to visit a showcase flat that they were showing to give social housing tenants the opportunity to see what their flat could look like if they bought it.

Social life

At college, I interacted much more with the friends of the other Anglophones. The Anglophones including myself were a seven-piece friendship group, and this in turn led to a fair bit of social contact with French students who were not members of my main group during break-times, including sitting together in the canteen. We also socialised at the many social events that took place in the evenings, which were very lively and great fun. Pubs and clubs might sound like an Aspie's worst nightmare. However, when the music is at a reasonable pitch, there is space to breathe and not too many annoying people, I can really enjoy myself. I'll be honest and say that there are often a few things that I find unpleasant to deal with, but I just tolerate the small unpleasant things in order to enjoy everything else. The social event highlight for me was going to watch one of the Austin Powers movies dressed for a Sixties evening. I dressed as Austin Powers and, to both my horror and amusement, looked more similar to him than I thought I would. I might be an Aspie, but I have my own unique sense of humour that people often appreciate and I know how to have fun when the opportunity arises.

In the halls, I often visited three of my neighbours, and they also often had friends round. Many of these were from

French parts of Africa and the Caribbean and had their own sub-culture and were very lively and friendly people. I used to sit in their respective rooms for hours on evenings and weekends, often taking time out to be alone and do some of my college work or revision and then going back again. I would hear so many new words and phrases popping up. At the beginning of the year, I used to listen extremely hard trying to make sense of what was being said. It tended often to be that I understood most of the words but only enough to grasp the concept of what was being said. Then over time, it became apparent that most of the words that I had not picked up were in fact words that I already knew, but didn't pick them up due to them being spoken very quickly and/or pronounced differently to the way I had assumed. On top of this, I picked up a lot of slang ways of saying things. By the end of the year, I was fluent and the sense of joy that this gave me was amazing.

Visiting places

Of course, no stay in France would be complete without visiting other parts of the country. I thoroughly enjoyed the customary trip to Paris, and all the more for doing it alone, and I also visited the tourist centres of Rouen, Etretat and Honfleur as well as the Normandy Bridge, all of which appear in iconic images of France. In July, having spent almost a year in a city in Normandy in the industrial north of France, I was now able to compare this with rural Auvergne towards the south of France. My hosts, who were a couple my French teacher at school had arranged for me to stay with just after I left school, lived in a typical sleepy French village, had a swimming pool in the back garden and a view of the beautiful Auvergne mountains. One Sunday evening, I was taken to a traditional fête in the nearest small town. Wooden tables had been set out on the riverside and a few hundred of us had a full and hearty traditional French meal and there was a lot of music, dancing and merriment. A lot of Aspies might not like the idea of a big social event like this, but I'm generally fine if I'm able to mostly observe. I didn't say much but listened a lot and thoroughly enjoyed myself. On the last weekend, I went to the other side of Normandy to stay in Caen with the family of one of the neighbours who I often visited in the halls. We visited the grounds of the two abbeys, a museum about the D-Day landings, which had happened nearby, and the local seaside resort of Caubourg close to Bayeaux, which is known for its tapestry.

My last moments in France

I was very sad after my friend and her father dropped me off at the Port of Caen as this was the end of my year abroad. I had to sit in the waiting area for a full two hours whilst the 1998 Football World Cup was on the television and had a really Aspie moment as I could have been the only grown man sitting in any French ferry port with a television switched on that evening to not be watching the game (it was France vs Brazil played on French turf). With my Aspie trait of separating logic from emotion, I've never appreciated why it's specifically football that everyone clubs together for. Twenty-two grown men chasing a hard round object around a muddy field. I just don't understand why that has to be the game that unites people worldwide. So, it doesn't interest me and as an Aspie who thinks for himself, I exercised my right to be me and not to watch it and not to follow the herd.

Back to reality

It took a while to readjust to life back home in England. Despite some issues, my year abroad had been a very fruitful and fulfilling experience. I experienced life in France in all its many forms, met several great people, learnt many things, became fluent in a foreign language and had the best time of my life, leaving me with happy, long-lasting memories. I still have a yearbook of the course, which I look at from time to time and remember the many people and situations and good times. My main regret is that, although I did have initial contact with some of the French students, this has gradually fizzled out. I have often thought that it would be interesting to make a visit to Le Havre and maybe go with family or friends to show them round, although I guess it would be hard to make other people appreciate the amazing things that happened behind those closed doors.

Ongoing benefits

There are several wonderful French people who will do anything for anyone, and there are others who are less pleasant and can be harsh, unrealistic and unfair, but when I'm in a foreign country, I just take people as they are, soak it all up and enjoy learning about their culture. If we get on, we get on, if we don't, we don't. I think that having a neurological difference myself helps me to appreciate cultural differences more, but perhaps having had this cultural experience where I learnt to expect the unexpected has also helped me to appreciate Aspie differences too. Not just how Aspies are different from the majority of people, but also how Aspies differ from one another, and this has helped me to empathise more with a wide variety of members that I've had to deal with as a result of running the UK-based website Aspie Village and its successful meet-ups for a decade.

Another thing is that the French have daily handshaking and kissing rituals in social-type environments. Whilst this was uncomfortable and exhausting especially at first (I'm still not especially fond of touch with someone who is not a partner), it has made it easier for me to cope with affection shown by some women. I sometimes initiate handshakes with men I meet for the first time at work as it can be the 'done thing' in some work situations. I'd prefer not to receive handshakes after the first meeting, but because it's so prolific in France, I can 'grin and bear it' it when it happens in my home country.

In terms of what effect my year in Le Havre has had in the intervening 16 years, after finishing university the following year, I have not had nearly as many brushes with the French language as I would have liked. Shortly after leaving university, I had a job interview 40 miles away from my home town to be a French speaker, but unfortunately got lost and did not make it to the interview. I was quite depressed about this for some time but I've since realised that I probably wasn't suited to the irregular pattern of hours. I simply couldn't get a break with the local company that employed several linguists because I was not outgoing enough or, if the job was as a French credit controller, didn't have the right accounting skills. I did, however, have a job for seven months as an administrator in a small translation company, and sometimes helped out with French translations.

That's the sum total of my experience of French or other languages in the workplace, and I do sometimes wish that this were not the case, especially when I find out through social networking what some of my old classmates from university are now doing.

However, keeping it positive, I do keep in touch with the language when I can through watching films, visiting French websites and even setting one of my computer games to French default setting, which made that even more fun to play. I guess that's part of the thinking outside the box which many Aspies can be excellent at when not under pressure. I have visited Paris three times in those 16 years. I think that almost certainly in the next three years, I should go back to another part of France, ideally further down south and possibly visit my long-term penfriend, with whom I've been in intermittent contact for 25 years. Visiting Quebec if I ever venture outside Europe could also be fun.

In the meantime, I have now become an intermittent member of a French language meet-up group. I have so far attended four times and each time has involved turning up, making sure it's the right group, saying 'Bonjour' to whomever is sitting closest to the first empty seat and just starting to chat away in French. The first time I went it felt as if I had returned to Le Havre and I don't think that I had ever felt so happy in a long time. In fact it happened at the height of a stressful period at work and was a wonderful tonic. The group is too far from my home to go often but now that I have found it I will go every few months perhaps for years to come. I also have French grammar books at home and when I find the time I will brush up a bit on that.

Measuring the glass

I don't remember whether Princess Diana's death played a part in inspiring me to enjoy the year, but when someone dies so young, it brings home the message of how precious life is and not to waste a single moment. Don't spend time dwelling on the past or fretting about what you're not good at.

Live in the here and now. There will be negatives in each person's life, but even people living in the direst of circumstances, such as living with an illness, can have positive experiences. If someone has been given one year to live, although that would be difficult to live with, they can still fill that year with an abundance of positive experiences. There is a well-known analogy that when a glass consists of half liquid and half nothing, the person who drinks from that glass either deems it to be half-full or half-empty. If their glass is half-empty, the individual is thinking in terms of what they do not have, and may measure their lot in life by what they do not have. They might waste a large proportion of their time worrying or complaining and seem to be eternally sceptical about people's motives. If the individual's glass is half-full, they probably focus on anything and everything that makes them and those around them happy and fulfilled in life.

The most cheerful people cannot be that way 24 hours a day, seven days a week. I'm a content person, but I'm not permanently happy, do have bad moods and sometimes lose my temper and, like everyone else, I have my off days. There are a lot of people out there who feel miserable just as much of the time as I feel content. I don't feel that it is healthy or realistic to assess almost everything in life in a negative way and certainly not to constantly put yourself down about what you don't have in life or have not done. If you are a good person with the best of intentions, then you automatically have something to be proud of, and you should feel proud every time you make the effort to do something good. All that you can do is try. Aspies can be prone to things not going quite as planned and being told that they did something wrong, sometimes nicely and sometimes not so nicely. I've had my own fair share of setbacks, but I've always just picked myself up and kept going, and whilst I'm not married, have no children and don't drive, my life has improved in so many ways. I've been working for a good employer for the past nine years and love the job that I do, have a good circle of friends (mostly from the Aspie world), run a website for Aspies in the UK and Ireland called Aspie Village, host successful meet-ups for its members, have co-written a few books, run a flat and enjoy my free time.

Advice for other Aspies

As I think the reader can probably tell by now, French is the one thing that really makes me happy. If I am able to give any Aspie-to-Aspie advice based on this chapter, it would be that whenever you feel stressed or unhappy, try to find the one thing that makes you feel happiest. This could be science-fiction novels, slapstick comedy, playing a musical instrument, mending a vehicle, making a model, spending time with your favourite animal or indeed a language. Finding a new hobby can often work. You could become so absorbed in it that you might even forget that you had felt under stress in the first place and might go to work one Monday morning in a great mood because you spent the weekend making something and feeling a sense of achievement once it was complete. Learning a new language is often good fun, and it's unlikely that that French teacher from school who made your life a misery is going to turn up. Learning things as an adult is a different experience from school.

A Sunday afternoon country ramble can be a winner due to the fresh air, exercise and beautiful views. You can find a club for that through an internet search. Many new hobbies and interests have clubs devoted to them. Other things, you could just find through the internet. Whatever it is that you come up with, the one thing that you should be trying to find is the one thing that makes you happy. If you try different things and they don't work for you, it doesn't matter because you can have fun looking for the activity that is the 'chosen one'. Also, if two or three things make you feel equally happy, then so much the better because you have two or three activities that can really lift your spirits when something has been getting you down, and you can truly have a positive experience and be very happy.

A few suggestions for a more positive lifestyle:

- Establish a healthy (not obsessive) routine that helps you to relax.

- Eat a healthy balanced diet.

- Walk outside for at least 20 minutes a day, longer where possible.

- Spend as much time outside as you are comfortable with.

- Take cardiovascular exercise as often as possible.

- Volunteer if you don't work.

- Take breaks from constructive activity.

- Be near nature when possible.

- Take opportunities to relax (e.g. read a book alone, or take a nice warm bath).

- Have a specific time in the day or week when you do something relaxing.

- Read books for tips on confidence, social skills and healthier lifestyles.

- Attend a local Asperger's/autism social or support group (not one for parents unless you want to).

- Read Asperger's/autism message boards where members share experiences and maybe join in.

- Search the internet for a hobby group (e.g. www. meetup.com) but always observe safety rules when meeting people online).

Chapter 10

The Story Behind a Story
My Novella – The Atlas Legacy

Colin Newton

Introduction by Luke Beardon

This is a fascinating chapter full of wit and humour outlining Colin's numerous excursions, most of which were undertaken as 'research' for his novel. Colin's style of writing is refreshing and bold, and in particular his personality seems to shine through. Colin demonstrates that while travel can be a stressful time for people with Asperger's syndrome (AS), it can also be a highly enlightening experience, and his tales are varied and intriguing. On reading this it strikes me that Colin could write reviews for holidays, such is the richness of his work! There is a lot of valuable information in this chapter relating to the lived experience of an individual; the way in which Colin uses travel to base his writing upon, and the way in which his writing progresses is a fascinating journey – and one that makes me want to read more!

This is the account of how my debut novella came to be written.

I've long been interested in ancient history and associated mysteries. I suppose I got into the subject at about age 12, when I read a book which analysed possible options for humanity to expand into space and which included a survey of possible evidence for alien contact in the past. One case that was cited as perhaps the strongest such evidence was the supposed 'Maps of the Ancient Sea Kings', which were studied in detail by Charles Hapgood in the 1950s. Hapgood's thesis was that certain medieval maps were somehow based on much more ancient source maps, which are now lost but which enabled medieval mapmakers to produce work that was more accurate than the methods of their time should have allowed.

Latitude is relatively easy to determine, but longitude famously is much harder and this was a major problem for sailors until the 1700s. It's well known that the British government offered a substantial prize, which was the incentive for John Harrison to eventually solve the problem by developing a reliable clock. One way to determine longitude is to be able to compare your local time with the time at a base location. Greenwich, London, was established as the base and so the difference between your local time and Greenwich Mean Time indicates your longitude. Alternatively, longitude can be determined from astronomical observations, but this is more difficult to do and attempts to make it practical eventually lost out to Harrison's chronometers.

Consequently maps from the 1500s and 1600s tend to be wildly inaccurate, except that some show portions that are clearly recognisable. One interesting example is a 1542 map by Jean Rotz. The original is held by the British Library, but copies used to be available from the Mary Rose gift shop at the historic dockyard in Portsmouth (on my most recent visit these copies were no longer being sold). The Mediterranean and all coasts as far north as southern England are drawn pretty well, but further north the inaccuracies are enormous. The proposed explanation for this is that southern Europe was mapped to a fair standard of accuracy during the last

Ice Age, whereas for regions that were then inaccessible due to the ice, later mapmakers had to use the less accurate techniques of their own day. This is backed up by Hapgood's identification of markings that he interpreted as indicating glaciers on other maps which he believed were derived from ancient sources.

However, Hapgood's thesis was complicated by the map most associated with his work, the Piri Re'is fragment from 1513, which shows the eastern coast of south America and then below it a coast running east–west. This is either a random doodle, or a representation of Antarctica centuries before it was officially discovered. So any theory to explain the hypothetical ancient source maps has to account for a curious mixture of glacial and ice-free conditions, such that Antarctica was accessible and worth mapping. Most analyses conclude that you need to postulate not one but two lost civilisations, or in some views alien visitations, active in two different time periods with different climates.

I was inclined to the view that the ancient source maps hypothesis was correct, just because the combining of accurate and inaccurate medieval mapping had to have some explanation, but was no better placed than anyone else to understand why. Because I have some interest in meteorology and climate, I realised that there was a possibility of explaining the mixture of climates if warm water currents such as today's Gulf Stream had existed in the appropriate places, but I knew of no historical climate evidence that fitted the idea. So I left it as an unexplained puzzle.

Around 20 years ago, I was reading what would be regarded as rather offbeat material, when I was startled to come across an analysis of ancient climate that had the potential to explain a mix of inland glaciers and relatively ice-free coasts, and moreover had them occurring at pretty much the same time. I'm not going to tell you what the answer is because that would be an enormous spoiler for the novella, but it completely revolutionised my thinking about ancient mysteries and I started to wonder how my insight could be presented to a wider audience.

As I don't have the credentials to get into the academic press, I started to think about presenting the theory in the form of a novel. I thought it might reach more people that way. I've been making up stories from early childhood and always wanted to try to get published some day.

Around this time my mum suggested going on a cruise. This was before Asperger's syndrome was widely recognised; my mum realised I was somehow different in an eccentric professor sort of way, but we didn't have a label for it. Actually she was probably on the autistic spectrum herself, with sensitivities to certain smells and types of noise, but no-one knew about such things then. She was concerned that I wouldn't be able to cope with looking after myself once she was no longer around to help me, and to someone of her generation the obvious solution was to find me a wife. But I was in a male-dominated industry, with limited outside interests, and it was very rare for me to meet a potential girlfriend, let alone overcome my social difficulties enough to speak to one. So Mum may have seen a cruise holiday as a last throw of the dice to find me a partner. She had always had poor health and possibly realised she had not much time left.

Anyway we looked up some brochures, and took a particular interest in a Bible Lands tour with a company specialising in the Christian market. I looked up their other destinations, thinking that I might try them if the first trip went well, and spotted that they fitted quite well with the sort of places I wanted to go to in order to research the novel which I was beginning to plan. So we booked – and then Mum caught an infection that was going around that winter, was admitted to hospital and shortly afterwards died. She expressed a deathbed wish that I would go ahead with the cruise anyway, and as that was still several months ahead there was time to get over the loss before travelling.

I'd never been away on my own except at university, but realised I was going to have to try it. I thought I would try a couple of days at a retreat centre to get used to the idea, but unexpectedly I learned of a weekend presentation by an Egyptologist whose work has a bearing on our understanding of biblical history. I only had a few days' notice of this; I was able to arrange a long weekend off work, but had no experience in booking B&Bs. I turned up in southeast London with an overnight bag in one hand and a list of late trains back home in the other. The event organisers were able to recommend a nearby B&B, and I dashed down there in the interval to secure a room for one night.

So that went okay, as did the retreat, except that I wildly underestimated the duration of a coach journey into London, missed my onward connection and eventually arrived after dinner had started. I began to find that going away from home reduced the pressure on me and so was beneficial rather than stressful.

For the cruise, my first ever overseas trip, a friend kindly offered to take me to the airport. This helped except that my obsessive compulsive disorder (OCD) kicked in after about a mile; I made him turn round and take me home to check that I hadn't forgotten a particular item. Later I learned to manage this by compiling an exhaustive list of everything I wanted to take with me, and ticking each item as it was packed. I stayed overnight at a Gatwick hotel, then took my first flight early on a foggy day that called to mind Théoden's departure 'From dark Dunharrow in the dim morning'.[1] I expected I would probably have a panic attack when we got close to take-off, and was relieved that this did not happen. In fact the first trip felt very much like a great adventure; by my third flight I was even finding that I could take a window

---

1   Tolkien, J.R.R. (1974) *The Return of the King*. London: Unwin Books, p.67.

seat without getting overcome by fear of heights. Later flights became progressively more stressful as I was more aware of what might go wrong.

We landed in Crete for transfer to the ship, and the whole week thereafter was more enjoyable than stressful. Kusadasi on the second day had the problem that I couldn't get off the ship without being harassed by salesmen. It seemed that 'no' was local slang for 'make me a better offer', and 'go and take a running jump off a cliff' would probably have translated as 'allow me a moment to consider your generous terms'. I hear, however, that this is no longer a problem, as they've all found gainful employment as telephone cold callers. I retreated to the ship until it was time for the official excursion.

The week then proceeded via Israel, Cyprus, Patmos and finally Athens for transfer to a flight home. At Jerusalem the early starts caught up with me. Whereas Jesus' first disciples had failed to last the course in Gethsemane, I nodded off briefly at the Garden Tomb. I ought to mention that Patmos is a beautiful island, largely unspoiled because the low rainfall means it can't support a large population. All the houses have tanks to maximise capture of rainfall, and even so they have to import supplies of water from the Greek mainland.

The following summer I was in Cornwall, staying at a guest house outside St Ives. I've found it generally helpful to stay at guest houses that focus on the Christian market, since it means I have at least one thing in common with the other visitors and so I'm less likely to be socially isolated. I was keen to work the mythology surrounding Lyonesse into my story. On the way over to the Scilly Isles, I found a map showing the land that is now underwater, displayed on the Scillonian III. I kept coming back to that and trying to think of a scenario, but nothing came to mind.

Back in St Ives, I signed up for a tour led by popular local character Harry Safari. Sadly Harry's tours are no longer running, but for a similar experience of less visited sites you can check out West Cornwall Tours. One of the stops was at an ancient hill fort above St Ives. As we came to the almost sheer eastern face of the fort, I looked south to St Michael's Mount, northeast to the Hayle estuary, and an ancient incident and a modern-day hunt for traces of it suddenly crystallised in my mind. This has been a recurring theme as I put the story together – I get stuck for ages, and then suddenly I get to a 'right time' when the next stage falls into place.

The next stop on the trail was the Italian Tyrol, which I've long been interested in. I had to get to Gatwick on my own, but at Verona I joined a group travelling on the same package. The flight was a late one and we made the coach transfer northward from Verona in darkness. Arriving at the hotel around midnight, I was startled to be served a delicious snack of Parma ham with fruit, whereas I expected to go straight to bed. At some stage early in my stay I must have talked enthusiastically of hoping to see the Bolzano museum, which was built to house the remains of 'Otzi the Iceman', though I don't recall the conversation. This led to several of the group taking the bus into Bolzano later in the week, and some of them told me that I'd persuaded them to do so. I suppose this must have been a rare example of an Aspie obsession managing not to bore the audience. However, I took quite a long time to check out all the exhibits, and only realised at the end that my companions had gone round much faster and had left me behind. I later transferred this circumstance into the back story of one of the novella's characters. Fortunately, I found them taking tea in a plaza elsewhere in the town. I'm not sure I could have managed the bus journey either way on my own because of the language issue, the particular problem for UK tourists in the Italian Tyrol is that it's bilingual (Italian and German) and so no-one has English as their second language, though some speak it as a third language. I speak a little French but stopped learning it before O level, a decision I now regret, and know no other modern language beyond odd words.

Otzi's role is only hinted at in my novella, but if I ever get to write the prequel, it will include my version and explanation of his final climb to death high in the Alps.

This was the first trip I'd done knowing that I had Asperger's syndrome – the diagnosis had been given a few months earlier. The tour group amounted to just under 20 people, and besides myself there was another single traveller who seemed to have a similar issue, though at the time I was yet to learn what signs to look for. For the highlight tours to Lake Garda and Venice, an older couple informally took on the responsibility of keeping an eye on both of us, which I found helpful. Remarkably, all the other members of the group had already been to Lake Garda and Venice, so it was just the four of us each time plus tourists from other hotels – mostly Germans. If I hadn't had the Asperger's diagnosis, I would probably have been too embarrassed to accept the help. At Sirmione at the southern end of Lake Garda, I felt confident enough to head out on my own to find a villa associated with the Latin poet Catullus. This however ended in failure, because we were there on the one day of the week on which it was closed. Fortunately Catullus had nothing to do with the story I was writing.

I came back from Italy with a sense that I had put the dream of the novella to the test and it was holding together. I started to look for a location that I could use to tie up all the threads. My first choice was a very exotic one. I'll keep that veiled for now because I still think it's a key place to look for traces of the ancient mapping process and I may want to use it later, but the cost of getting there and the limited possibilities of exploring it weighed against it. In the end I settled on Malta for the conclusion.

So I booked a trip to Malta – and the stress-related eczema that had plagued me since my mum died flared up again. Instead of going to Malta, I found I was hospitalised for a few days of intense treatment. This was the second of three such episodes. Once again, the project was blocked until the timing was right.

As I was restricting myself to travelling with the same holiday company each time, for the sake of familiarity with the procedures, it was some time before I could make another attempt to get to Malta. Meanwhile I managed a few days on Crete, without much thought of using it for the book, but just for a rest as I recovered from the eczema treatment. However, I had a bit of inspiration while visiting the port of Hania on a tour, and spent my lunch-break there plotting out a chase sequence. This was a particularly enjoyable scene for me to write, as I had the bad guy take a tumble into the harbour at the end. In working through the rest of the chapter I resolved an issue that had been bothering me: how to get three people from very different backgrounds and viewpoints, each of whom had a necessary part to play in solving the mystery, to actually team up plausibly.

Then came the delayed trip to Malta. By then I was struggling with stomach issues, which had been worsened by the side-effects of the eczema treatment, and which eventually led to me discovering that I had a rare food intolerance, as well as ideally having to avoid certain fats and fruits. But I got around enough to come up with the location I was looking for in which to set the climax of the story. I came home with a feeling that it was now time to pull the whole story together.

I already had a few chapters drafted, and managed to put together some more. It soon became clear that the story was shorter than a full-length standard novel. My writing has always been concise, and it's very difficult for me to put together flowery descriptive passages or to build complex characterisations. It's probably a variation on the typical Asperger's pattern of being very good at some things and poor at others, but all within the same field of writing. I also write poems and I think I'm extremely good at fitting words to a suitable rhythm, but poor at some of the other skills poets are supposed to use. I regard my style as close to the ancient roots of poetry, in putting together words in a memorable way so that key elements of a culture's history were retained in oral memory. It should possibly be described as 'chanting' rather than poetry.

People who know me will not be surprised that the novel is strongly rooted in my Christian worldview. For that reason I was clear from the outset that I was going to approach only specialist Christian publishers. This, however, greatly limited my choice as there is a very limited UK market for fiction written from a specifically Christian standpoint – though it sells well in the USA.

Before submitting the story, I tried asking a few friends to review it for me. I have limited confidence in my abilities at most things, and needed a bit of reassurance. Also I was concerned that my autistic way of looking at things might cause me to write certain elements of the story in unrealistic ways, particularly the interplay of characters. Unfortunately, the people who agreed to review it mostly let me down, such as by never managing to finish the story. At the other end of the scale, there was one who became so enthusiastic about the story that she completely failed to critique it in a useful way. I did get some useful feedback from my brother, some of which got incorporated into the final version of the story.

I then tried a few submissions to publishers, but got nowhere. I received mixed advice on whether the story should be targeting the adult or young adult market. A highly qualified acquaintance suggested it was suitable for teenagers, and I think that a high-functioning young Aspie with the appropriate special interest would understand and enjoy it, but a children's publisher I approached was certain that the average young adult wouldn't read it.

After that I wasn't sure how to proceed. I left the whole project on hold for a while, and then found that because it had a near-future setting, several passages were out of date and had to be revised. I also gradually became more capable of doing my own critique, recognising the weak points and eventually managing to replace them with passages that worked better. The final revision occurred with a last-minute discovery that a formerly flourishing hotel was now derelict – I hurriedly converted its role in the story to that of being the site of an archaeological dig. I've noticed that I'm still more familiar with the pre-revision version of the story than the final text, so a question focused on a recently revised aspect is liable to confuse me.

Meanwhile, there was a new player in the Christian publishing market, one which is far more open to new authors. I finally got round to doing a submission to Onwards and Upwards, and was delighted to receive a swift positive response. I think they managed to get the story reviewed for a decision by someone with an appropriate specialist knowledge, rather than a commissioning editor with only general knowledge. The downside of finding a publisher that takes risks with new authors is that I had to put up some money myself, but I am getting help, particularly with marketing, which would otherwise be difficult for me as an autistic person. They've also supplied some useful light touch editing, prompting me to clear up a few loose ends in the plot, but being prepared to accept my judgement on one or two occasions when I've said: 'No, I wrote it this way because...' Self-publishing would not have worked for me. The book was published in autumn 2015. Further information can be found on my website (www.atlaslegacy.co.uk).

The Atlas Legacy
A novel by
COLIN NEWTON

Chapter 11

My London Marathon Experience
Walking into a New Day

Dominic Walsh

Introduction by Luke Beardon

This chapter is a brilliant depiction of what can be achieved with a level of determination and goal setting. Dominic describes how he trained for walking a marathon distance for charity, followed by the experience of doing the walk itself. The writing is littered with insights into how Asperger's syndrome (AS) impacts upon Dominic in a whole host of ways; what stands out for me is the sheer determination and commitment Dominic displayed throughout his training and during the event itself. I sometimes wonder whether endurance events are well suited to people with AS; many of the characteristics that are associated with AS could be useful in terms of being driven to a physical goal – the repetitive training, the time spent on one's own, the clear-cut goal, the focus – these are often aspects of life that perhaps relate well to AS. Whether this is the case or not, Dominic writes in an inspirational way about his own journey and selflessness in fundraising for charity, and shows what can be done with the right temperament and support.

My name is Dominic Walsh, I'm 29 years old and I was diagnosed with traits of Asperger's syndrome when I was 11. These traits include difficulty understanding implied meanings in social interactions, difficulty finding my way around when I am away from home or in a place I do not know, intense interests that have included Games Workshop and *Doctor Who*, and obsessive thoughts, usually along the lines that I have upset someone in a social interaction or that I am becoming a horrible person. Since I was diagnosed I have improved my ability to interact socially with the help of friends, family and carers, and I have learned to find my way to places that I have never been to before.

In 2012 I walked a half marathon to raise money for Cancer Research UK. I did this to lose weight and to do something for charity. In 2014 I didn't have much to do after the drama group I went to finished and I was starting to experience negative and obsessive thoughts. I thought about walking another half marathon and I suggested this to my carer Neil. There was some indecision about whether I wanted to walk another marathon but eventually I decided to do it. Neil and I were travelling to the National Autistic Society's (NAS) social group in Manchester in May when we discussed the marathon. Neil asked if I wanted to walk another half marathon or the full marathon and initially I chose the half marathon. I couldn't get rid of the feeling that I was taking the easy option, which seemed to be reflected in the responses from Neil and some of the guys we spoke to at the meet-up. While we were waiting for the bus back from the NAS meet-up I decided I would attempt the full marathon. I was nervous, and I wondered if I could actually walk 26.2 miles when I had found the half marathon a challenge. I told Neil that I was going to try and walk the full marathon and he seemed impressed.

As we travelled back to my flat on the bus, Neil talked about training for the full marathon. I have a circuit of roughly two miles around the town I live in that I walk most evenings. When I trained for the half marathon my carer

Stuart and I worked out that eight 'laps' of the circuit would be the distance I would have to walk on the night of the half marathon. I said that 16 laps around my circuit would be the length of the full marathon and Neil told me to try walking at a fast pace. If I could walk five times around my circuit, and then rest, then another five laps, and then rest, and then a final five, I would be ready for the full marathon. The first time I walked five laps of my circuit I was completely drained. My legs ached and wobbled and I felt too tired to do anything else. When I walked the distance again I felt less tired at the end because I took a litre of water with me. By the fifth or sixth time I did this walk I wasn't tired.

Cancer Research UK set up a JustGiving page for me, which I linked to on Facebook, Deviantart and OKCupid. I had raised £180 when I walked the half marathon so Neil and I set a fundraising target of £360. I said in one status update that if I raised more than this amount I would walk the marathon dressed as the Eleventh Doctor. I did not raise over £360 so this did not happen. Over time I was able to walk 15 times around my circuit with rests on the benches in Timperley village. Often I would start my training late in the day, or I would need to go to the toilet while I was walking, so I was unable to walk as many laps as I wanted to. During my final week of training I was able to walk without needing the toilet and resting when I needed to.

On Friday 26 September my carer Ola and I took a tram from Timperley metro station to Manchester Piccadilly. At the train station we were given free stain removing kits by a promoter and we were asked if our picture could be taken with them. The train journey was uneventful and after four hours we were in London. Ola and I travelled on the London Underground to our hotel near Old Billingsgate, which was where the marathon finished. I was reminded of the bit in *Neverwhere* when Richard watches the faces of the other passengers on the Underground and wonders what they are thinking. I hoped I could see the *Neverwhere* bench while we were in London but I did not. Ola and I checked into the hotel and then we went out to eat at a Chinese restaurant that Ola knew. Ola had lived in London before moving to Manchester and he was a gigantic help because he knew where everything was. I'm very grateful to Ola for coming with me to London and helping me.

The next day we found out where the marathon started and we bought some safety pins to attach my walking number to my t-shirt. We went back to the hotel and I rested and read my book. Eventually it was time to set off. We caught the bus to Southwark Park where the London Shine walk started, and I hung back in a café area for a while because I didn't like the noise that the DJ and music were making. At quarter to nine I decided to go to where the marathon participants had to assemble and Ola said he would see me later when I finished. I walked through the park, through the gate marked Striders and I was given a flashing wrist band that didn't flash. After about 25 minutes the Striders were asked to move to their gate and I did so. When the marathon started I was in a giant crush of people and I was only able to walk very slowly but as the walk continued I could eventually move at my own pace.

When I walked the half marathon I was part of the group of entrants that were called Strollers, which meant that we walked at the slowest pace. This time I was in the group that were called Striders, who walked faster than Strollers but slower than Power walkers. I kept thinking to myself 'Push forward' and I walked at a relatively quick pace. I took some photos of London at night on my phone as I walked, which I put on Facebook. There were pitstops dotted around the walk where we could rest and go to the toilet. I stopped and sat on some steps where I ate a sandwich I had bought earlier that day. By the time I was between the second and third pitstop I was angry with the volunteers who said that the pitstop was 'just around the corner'. I managed to get to it and I went to the toilet there, which we had to queue up for. I ate my second sandwich, rested a bit and set off.

The first twenty miles of the marathon were not a problem for me, but by the last six I was tired, aching and I really wanted to sit down. Fortunately the route took us past many benches where I was able to sit and rest. At the fourth pitstop we were given biscuits and I sat down and counted to a hundred to relax my mind and body. I then got up and kept walking. Roads were a bit of a problem to me because I have this thing about road safety and I will not cross unless the green man is showing, except on roads I know really well. Whenever I passed a sign that told us how many miles we had walked I raised my index finger aloft. It's just something I do when I complete one lap of my training walks. As I began to ache more and more I kept repeating to myself 'I can do it, I can do it, I can do it' over and over and over again as I walked.

After nearly nine hours it was light again and I took some amazing photos of the River Thames and the London skyline in the morning. Somebody walking down the street in the morning overheard me saying 'I can do it' and asked how many miles I still had to go. I told him I had 0.2 miles left to walk and he gave me a high five and wished me luck. I crossed another road and walked down and around a winding street before coming to the finish line. I walked up some steps into a black felt corridor studded with stars and I came out at the finish. Ola was there and he took a photo of me next to the finish line. I walked across it and through some lanes created by metal barriers where a nice man gave me a medal for completing the marathon. I couldn't believe I had actually done it but I was really glad that I did. I had a cup of tea and sat down on the floor, and then I texted my mum. Ola and I then walked back to our hotel, where we began to get ready to leave. Training for the marathon gave me something to focus on and completing it has given me more confidence. I'm very glad I walked the full marathon and I'm incredibly grateful to the guys who have sponsored me and to Ola for going with me to London.

Chapter 12

In an Economic Climate When the Most Able in Society Are Having Difficulty Finding Work, What Chance Do Those with Disabilities Have?

Tony's Journey

Maggie

Introduction by Luke Beardon

This is an emotive chapter that outlines the very real issues that some individuals will face in education, especially when their autism is either not recognised and/or not supported. The fact that Tony has emerged from negative experiences to continue into adulthood with a new venture of self-employment is testament to what can be achieved with the appropriate support mechanisms in place.

Employment can be a tough environment for anyone, and there are clearly additional difficulties that many autistic individuals may face. Being self-employed can be a fabulous alternative for some people on the spectrum, as indicated in this chapter. Being one's own 'boss' without having to engage with colleagues can be extremely rewarding; as noted within the chapter, though, there are also aspects of being self-employed that can be a challenge. It's refreshing to read a chapter such as this that, in the main, articulates major problems for the individual – and yet, ultimately, is seen as culminating in a positive. This is a great example of the resilience that can be found in an individual – not an uncommon characteristic to be found amongst those on the spectrum!

According to statistics published by the foundation for people with learning disabilities, 'there are an estimated 800,000 adults with learning disabilities of working age, of which fewer than 7 per cent have a paid job, often a part time one'.[1]

In an economic climate when the most able in society are having difficulty finding work, what chance do those with disabilities have?

Many parents with children on the autistic spectrum will know only too well about the angst that is associated with every stage of their child's development.

First there is the fight to have them diagnosed, the fight to find the right school placement and the level of support necessary to see them through the educational system and indeed to manage the everyday demands of what living on the spectrum means, and then comes the question of work.

Maggie is an undiagnosed dyslexic mother of four, who cares for two teenagers diagnosed with high-functioning autism spectrum disorder (ASD) and co-occurring learning difficulties. At the age of 48, she has only just been diagnosed with Asperger's syndrome herself and has battled

---

1   Foundation for People with Learning Disabilities (n.d.) 'Self-employment: In business.' Available at www.learningdisabilities.org.uk/our-work/employment-education/in-business, accessed 15 August 2016.

many difficulties throughout her life with relationships, independent living and employment issues.

Despite her difficulties she decided to start her own business from home four years ago in order that she could be there to care for her children's needs, but also to give her an interest, beyond care. She also regularly contributes on forum discussions, helping other parents with children on the spectrum.

Maggie discusses her journey with her two autistic sons. A common reoccurring theme that features on many community forums is that children on the spectrum with high-functioning autism and associated difficulties often seem to cope with their school day with little incident and then all hell breaks loose when they walk out of the school gates.

Any parent familiar with this facet of a child's life with ASD can be forgiven for worrying about whether this pattern of behaviour will continue throughout their child's life, and I am one such parent. Most parents also report a marked improvement in their child's behaviour during school holidays or periods off school, but they also worry that if their children have difficulty managing in certain environments when young, how will they cope in the working world?

My sons, Roy and Tony (not their real names), are both high-functioning, but had some pretty traumatic experiences in the primary education system.

Roy went on to a specialist primary school for those with dyslexia and ASD for a while, but following his brother Tony's diagnosis and some serious soul-searching, both then moved on together, to a mainstream secondary where they had statements and were extremely well supported. This was perhaps the best phase in their educational journey.

Once their statements ended at age 16, however, both boys' experiences were vastly different.

Roy went to an autism aware mainstream college to study his A levels and has since gone on to become an ambassador for autism for students and staff at the college. He receives good support there, yet he still suffers severe and frequent ill-health with the stress levels he experiences in education.

Tony went on to a practical college with a round journey of some 80 miles a day, but received little or no support in his education for his learning difficulties. Despite having a Learning Disability Assessment, which clearly outlined the provision he needed to access education, he was given no support. His self-esteem was further compromised when the college dropped him down from a level 3 diploma, to a level 2 certificate in the subject he chose.

There was no justification for this action, as he'd already achieved this level in previous years, as a day-release student at college. The course level was nowhere near the level commensurate with his intelligence and proved to be a total waste of an academic year for him. The tragedy was that it was a subject he excelled in and also his special interest, which was machinery.

At the time I couldn't understand the college's stance. Surely, it would have been better to provide the support the pupil needed and have greater achievement for the college and pupil at a higher level, than to drop the student down to levels that were below his intelligence. When I challenged the lack of support, I was informed that the college's method was more in keeping with what went on in life. There was no support in mainstream life and their approach was how it was in the real world! To say I was floored was an understatement.

Then I realised that it was not just about the cost factor involved in supporting those with special needs, but also about the discriminatory attitude towards pupils with disabilities that was clearly endemic at the college itself. Sadly, in talking with other parents across the country, it became clear that our experience was not an isolated incident.

It's common for autistic children's anxiety to grow and behaviour to become worse as they move up the academic ladder, particularly if a child is not well supported, but the backlash from such a poor attitude toward my son's disabilities was horrendous. In fact his further educational experience rates as one of the worst academic years he's ever endured. And to have happened in a subject that had consumed him for most of his life was a double blow.

Meltdowns of epic proportions ensued. Also, more frequent episodes of night terrors, bed-wetting, aggression, depression and some social choices that left him highly vulnerable. As his mother I was sleeping very little of a night and could barely function during the day with all the worry. I was exhausted with the increased level of behavioural issues I had to cope with and near breakdown myself.

Following our complaint to the college and an extremely underhand act where they sat my son down and made him provide signatures against dates for provision he never received, the decision was made to walk away from the college and education. He became a NEET (Not in Education, Employment or Training).

At the beginning of the summer holidays I had a tired and broken child with little trust and an aversion to education, which will probably be lifelong. We spent much of the time in the early months reassuring him and trying to help him look at options for the future. His results arrived, but he discarded them immediately. He'd achieved a certificate of distinction in all areas, but for him the reward was empty. He knew he was capable of the diploma he'd applied for and his high results at the lower level of certificate study further reinforced that.

Having said that, the summer was as calm and peaceful as we'd ever known it. After 13 years of primary, secondary and a brief brush with further education, his educational journey had ended. The system had chewed him up and spat him out and yet, with its end, came a sense of relief that as a family we'd never witnessed before.

So what now?

Any parent facing such anxiety and behavioural issues with a child can develop a sense of foreboding about what the future will hold and whether this is the calm before the storm. It can't continue surely? Yet again I'm guilty of such thoughts and had real reservations about the next phase in my son's life. We were given two choices. He found a job or he signed on.

Reams of job applications and refusals later, it slowly dawned on Tony that the work environment posed many of the barriers he'd encountered in education. Despite constant reassurance from his family his morale began to slip further as the months went by.

Once again, after much soul searching, we decided to take a course that on the face of it appeared quite controversial and frankly a little barking and that was that my son needed to work for himself!

Really?

My son is a kind soul. He's a very visual learner and great with mechanical repairs. He's desperate to do things right and has persevered through some pretty horrendous times; having said that, he also has some pretty limiting difficulties.

My son cannot wake himself. In fact on average it takes approximately 45 minutes to get him out of bed each morning. He's often up all night due to his sleep difficulties, but will no longer take his melatonin. He has severe dyslexia and can't read or write very well. Despite his practical skills, he cannot cook a meal from scratch or judge how long to microwave food, and, as you would assume, struggles greatly with social communication and needs much encouragement and reassurance. He's heavily reliant on his family to prompt him, get him around and to help him manage his everyday living.

What were we thinking? At least, that's what everybody asked.

The local Youth Employment Service said they'd never mentored a 16-year-old with learning difficulties who wanted to become self-employed before and they were not sure how to help him or even who to recommend that could. However, they did agree to support him in an application for a theory test to drive, once he turned 17.

As is the case for many parents with children who have learning difficulties or disabilities, it was clear this venture would have to be parent driven, so it left us no other option than to search for solutions ourselves. We found a free local business enterprise start-up course and against great opposition (my son thought it was going to be like an educational setting) we enrolled on it. We never mentioned his learning difficulties to the tutor, but I took notes and Tony sat through the whole day enthralled by what the business advisor had to say. I could see lightbulbs going off in his head in all directions and he fired ideas for me to write down as they popped into his mind. When he left the building I knew this was the direction he wanted to go in.

We've started slowly and in manageable, measured steps. Each day brings a new challenge and we discuss the best way to tackle it.

Despite his difficulties, he seems to be coping. Naturally, he needs huge support for all the written elements, bookings, time management and daily organising, but his practical skills with machinery seem to be carrying him through.

He controls the hours he wants to do, so overload is limited and he's doing something he enjoys. For the first time he feels his life is manageable and he's happy. Does he need constant support? Absolutely! Will he continue to need support? Probably! Will he encounter problems in the future? Almost definitely! Yet the transformation in him since eliminating the pressure cooker of education is palpable and not one I would have believed possible.

ASD is a hidden disability and for that reason it can be argued that it's all the more challenging for those who suffer with it. In a society that views disability as a visual thing, the impact and prejudice for those with invisible disabilities is often more profound. People have huge difficulty in understanding the disparity between how you speak or appear and how you struggle with everyday tasks in life. As a child, having difficulties is often tolerated much more than it is as an adult. If you are an adult on the spectrum, life can be pretty tough.

The truth is that children with autism grow up to become adults with autism. Autism is neurological condition that will impact on every element of their lives, but that doesn't mean that those on the spectrum who are able, can't become valued and contributing members of society.

Many, like myself, have lived their whole lives undiagnosed and have struggled unsupported through life, yet have had to look at alternative ways to contribute to society, faced with such prejudicial barriers and personal circumstance.

For the more severe among those with ASD, support is essential, yet with that support they continue to amaze us with their tenacity, perfectionism, determination and perseverance.

I'm a great advocate for education, but it's fair to say many youngsters' experiences are traumatic and they aren't being supported well enough to attain the best they can, which does leave doubt in parents' minds as to how they will cope in the future.

The fact remains that the working world is filled with undiagnosed ASD sufferers who decide to run their own business when faced with the prejudicial door closing of educational establishments, employment offices and employers. Some even leave school with no qualifications, yet the self-employed individual, cottage industry or small business is considered the backbone of our economy.

Those with a diagnosis are no different to those who don't have one and they should be able to access the same opportunities. In my view limiting someone to just two choices in this economic climate is no choice at all. Self-employment is not for everyone, but it's an option that should at least be put on the table.

It's early days for Tony, but my sense of pride in him is only overshadowed by the level of happiness I've witnessed in him. He still has his meltdowns, but with the volume turned way down. The future is a whole lot brighter.

Chapter 13

Loyal Companions
*Animals Can Teach Us All a Lot
about Happiness and Acceptance*

Debbie Allen

Introduction by Dean Worton

I've known Debbie for many years and have enjoyed
reading everything she has ever written, which is all
so fresh and honest. What you see is what you get.
Like so many on the spectrum she has had a lot of
setbacks but she just keeps going by filling her life
with positive experiences.

Animals can create the perfect pathway for
people with Asperger's syndrome (AS) to interact
not just with the animals but also with other people
through a shared love of animals, providing an
easy talking point. They are a calming influence
and do not judge the person with autism on their
differences. If anything, based on accounts I've read
on AS discussion forums, it's possible that some
domestic animals are overall more receptive to
people on the autistic spectrum, as though they pick
up on something gentle and trustworthy in their
nature. Maybe animals understand autistic people
better than predominant neurotypes (PNTs) do.
They do not judge them on their social differences
and can make wonderful companions. I would
recommend getting a pet to anyone with AS who is

allowed to have one, and, if not, getting involved
with animals through, for example, volunteering at
a stables or learning to ride a horse.

My diagnosis didn't come until I was in my mid-forties so I
was unaware of having Asperger's syndrome for most of my
younger years. I was, however, very aware of being different
to others around me. As a young child I always felt as though
the one thing that I had going for me was being a 'gentle'
type. I think I was told this often by my mother and others
were told this too. Maybe I was suited to what was to become
my main hobby throughout my life – caring for small animals
and birds.

As a child at primary school I was so excited when my
brother was trusted with the task of caring for the class
gerbil for a week during school holidays. It turned out he
wasn't even vaguely interested in it so I eagerly took over
his job of feeding it, changing the drinking water daily and
cleaning out the cage. I must have spent hours just watching
the gerbil and its antics.

When the pet was to be returned to the class I felt very sad
and at a loose end. My parents decided to allow me to have
my own gerbil and took me to a pet shop to buy one along
with a bright red metal cage, which I can vividly remember.
I became very interested in these friendly small animals and
spent a great deal of time reading up on them, borrowing as
many books from the library as I could.

This first gerbil lived a good long life but when it died I
decided to replace it with two gerbils, so they would have
company of their own kind. I didn't like the idea of a pet
being on its own without another of its kind for company.
Throughout my school days I kept gerbils and spent a great
deal of time watching their behaviour and caring for them.
They also gave me a real sense of responsibility and taught
me that I was able to take care of another living thing.

Watching and studying them provided a super means of relaxation after the stress of sitting in a classroom all day. They gave me something of interest to talk about to my class mates too, and if anyone ever came into the house I could show them the gerbils.

At about the age of ten my parents bought a cocker spaniel puppy for the family and we named him Brandy. I cannot imagine what life would have been like without a dog in the family. We all got so much pleasure from him and I would often come home from school and take him to the park for long walks. Having a dog meant that people spoke to me when I was out and about, and it was easier to make conversation when I was talking to the person about Brandy.

I continued to keep my gerbils and in my teens I bought a pair of female gerbils as usual since I worried that two males wouldn't get along so well. Little did I know that the pet shop owner had made a mistake: instead of two males he had sold me one male and a pregnant female! I was totally taken aback as I cleaned out their cage one day and spotted four baby gerbils in the nest. They had obviously been there for a few days when I saw them and although hairless were quite chunky and healthy looking but still bald and blind. I had always dreamed of breeding gerbils but the text books were full of scare stories so I had decided only to keep same sex pairs just in case some horror would happen and the babies would be eaten alive or goodness knows what. From this moment on I began breeding gerbils.

I was about 15 at the time and it wasn't too long before new coat colours in gerbils started appearing in the pet shops. Up until then they only had been available in the wild colour of speckled reddish brown known as 'agouti'. I was lucky to be keeping gerbils at this time as one by one many new colour combinations were being bred. Some of them were imported from other countries by enthusiasts who could afford to pay quarantine fees.

As the years went by and I left school and started working, I met others who were interested in keeping and breeding gerbils as well as other small animals. I decided to learn about coat colour genetics and it wasn't long before I could predict which colours would appear in the litters that my gerbils had. My young gerbils were always popular with pet shop owners and if I took them to small animal shows there would be plenty of people happy to buy them from me. I had quite a number of breeding pairs by this time.

Travelling around the UK every few months to small animal events was such fun and meant I could learn a little about the various towns and cities in England where I had never been before. The people who I met at these events were always friendly and very down to earth. As well as gerbil enthusiasts I met mouse, rat, hamster, guinea pig and rabbit breeders. I enjoyed seeing how enthusiastic the people who engaged in their hobbies were. Mouse breeding seemed to attract mainly retired people. I was in my early twenties at the time and thought it seemed a great hobby for someone whose job had come to an end. I later found out that mouse breeding in the north of England was the equivalent of pigeon racing in Scotland. Rat breeders, like the gerbil club, consisted of a mixture of all age groups as did the hamster club. The rabbit breeders always seemed to keep themselves separate from the other clubs. I don't think they had much time for the breeders of other small pets apart from the guinea pigs or cavies as they were known. Two of the people who often travelled with myself and my friend were rabbit breeders, though, and they were lovely and friendly. I am pretty sure that some of these animal enthusiasts were undiagnosed Aspies.

I usually enjoyed looking around the merchandise stands as much as anything else at the animal shows and would always treat myself to something like a T-shirt or brooch. Later I became interested in raising funds for the gerbil club and was usually involved in some type of money-making escapade like 'guess the teddy bear's birthday'.

This hobby helped me so much in gaining some confidence in myself. I became confident at travelling by myself within the UK and had the opportunity to socialise with others who had a strong interest in common with me. I could be part of something where people were also lighthearted and enjoyed having a laugh. Sometimes the members of the gerbil club would stay overnight in a B&B and take over the whole place.

When I was at school I had a voluntary weekend job caring for animals in a veterinary surgery. I didn't really enjoy this though as the staff who worked there were never very friendly towards me. Also, I was very nervous of cats and one of my tasks was to change the newspapers in the cages of cats that were recovering from operations. I was better at coping with the dogs as the place where I interacted with them was a boarding kennels so they were not grumpy like the cats, and, having owned a dog for a while, I felt more confident handling them. I also helped the vet in the consulting room and learned a lot about animals in the short time I was there. For a few years I studied part time at college, learning about animal sciences such as physiology, anatomy and animal husbandry, and got really good results in these subjects.

The family dog lived a long life and an interest I took up when he was about ten years old was clipping dogs. I travelled to England and took a two-week residential full-time course on dog clipping and grooming. It was quite a nerve wracking thing for me at the time, but often in the long run it is taking part in activities like this which have given me confidence, and the knock-on effect has made them really worthwhile. I was based in a grooming and clipping parlour for dogs in Manchester and worked there full time for two weeks learning the basics of clipping the most common breeds of dogs. Most of the people on the course were planning on opening their own grooming parlours and this was an eye-opener for me. I had only planned on taking the course out of interest and so that I could groom the family cocker spaniel. I bought the clippers necessary for the task along with a few brushes, scissors, combs and nail clippers, and from then on I groomed the family pet.

In my mid-twenties I became interested in keeping budgies. One of my workmates had bought one as a pet for her children, who I regularly babysat for. After a while I decided to get myself a budgie as they seemed such funny characters. To this day I have kept budgies, always in pairs, and when one member of the pair dies I get a young one to go with it so they are never lonely. Usually an older one left on its own will accept a very young bird as a companion but would fight with another adult. I just love watching them and they provide me with so many laughs along with helping me to get up in the mornings. In the winter months especially they are so cheerful with their whistling.

I love talking to people about my pets, but have to really limit what I say as so few people are interested in animals and especially birds. I was very lucky in having a colleague in my last job who had a female budgie which she loved so much. To this day I send her the occasional email about my budgies and their antics, and she cared for them once when I went on holiday. They were so much noisier than the one she had kept though and I think she and her husband were glad to see the back of them. I now have an Aspie friend who adores animals of all kinds and she cares for my budgies when I go on holiday. She also enjoyed keeping small pets but doesn't have any now so my two birds are quite a novelty when they arrive for their holidays with her.

I think keeping pets is a great thing for people who have autism and Asperger's syndrome, and that they can make a big difference to the quality of the person's life. They are not only great for children but also adults, and I'm sure there are many elderly undiagnosed Aspies out there whose main companion is their pet.

Chapter 14

Celebrating the Autism Spectrum

PJ Hughes

Introduction by Dean Worton

PJ is a role model for others with Asperger's syndrome
(AS). He has clearly had a lot to deal with in his life,
but he holds down paid employment, writes, speaks
and studies part time at degree level as well as being
involved with the National Autistic Society, and all
with a mobility issue. He certainly keeps busy and
is a very productive member of society. To class his
AS as normal is entirely the right approach. Perhaps
it would be helpful if the predominant neurotype
(PNT) majority were no longer classed as 'normal',
because whilst it might be normal for the vast
majority of the population to be PNT, it is equally
normal for 1 per cent to have an autism spectrum
disorder, and they should not be questioned for
being the way they are unless they are physically or
emotionally harming themselves or others.

Learning a foreign language can be good for
people with AS as it's a skill most English speakers
don't have beyond the basics, which can be a real
confidence booster, and if the student enjoys the
language they can almost become a different person

whilst speaking it. It could also come in handy in the right workplace.

My name is PJ Hughes and I was diagnosed with Asperger's syndrome in 1999. And, yes, PJ is my real first name. While I was given a different name as a baby, I changed it to PJ after I was diagnosed and as a result of the diagnosis. Initially, PJ was a nickname obtained while at polytechnic as it then was. Now, my old name, as far as I am concerned, is a term of abuse. I currently work, at the time of writing, in the public sector. I am also a speaker and writer on the autistic spectrum as well as being involved with the National Autistic Society, including having been a trustee. While having studied mathematical subjects to university level when I was younger, I also have a postgraduate certificate in Asperger's syndrome obtained from Sheffield Hallam University and I am currently studying for a degree in French part time. I am hoping to include some modules in Spanish in this course as well.

I have often noted that getting a diagnosis turned my life the right way up. It explained why other people were peculiar and strange in their behaviour! It helped describe why being alone is perfectly normal. It helped me put into perspective what I liked and disliked and so on. However, it is not without its problems owing to the number of people who think it is their place to make suggestions and stupid comments, all of which make things really awful. When I got my diagnosis, as I described in my book, *Reflections: Me and Planet Weirdo* (2007, Chipmunka), I noted that this was like coming out of a walking coma.

At school, my main strengths, probably not surprisingly, were mathematical. Given the nature of the type of syllabus at school at the time, there was little scope to fully realise what the range of my real strengths were. I also seem to remember rumblings of being good at French. The biggest challenges, however, were a lack of diagnosis and a very negative childhood, both at school and at home. They were the overriding reasons why I left London. Surviving school and scraping the grades to get to polytechnic, as it was then, was enough to escape. Since my diagnosis, I have been studying part time at both college and university (as well as working). I did A levels in film studies and music and have been studying languages (French, Italian and Spanish) through to university level. These subjects are, I believe, what I am better at and are something I would like to continue. Certain employment does make it tougher to fully focus on these subjects. Hence, I have to (learn to) juggle a number of activities and, rather frustratingly, have to accept that I won't be able to fully concentrate as much as I would like. Having said that, the course I am doing at the university (correct at the time of writing) enables me to include modules that are close to my interest in films.

For me, being an Aspie is perfectly normal and acceptable. The way I do things works for me despite the challenging behaviour from others, who ask questions like 'Why do you do this?', 'Why do you do that?', or state 'I don't understand', absolutely none of this being positive or constructive! Despite all the negative input, I try and implement as many of my decisions as possible. Sometimes I have to ask for some help, however uncomfortable. I often do things alone for the simple reason that it is usually far easier.

A few years after I was diagnosed I started to become a personal perspective speaker and writer on autism. As mentioned above I have had a book published called *Reflection: Me and Planet Weirdo*, and have been a regional councillor since 2007 and a trustee at the National Autistic Society (2011–2014). I have also take part in research, often at Cambridge University. This has been useful in coming to a personal understanding of the subject. One of my proudest moments was being invited to 10 Downing Street as part of the 50-year celebrations of the National Autistic Society.

Whenever I need help to do something, it works well when there's good communication. That way, I know what's happening, when and where. On the other hand, whenever people try and make suggestions, disaster is a very real outcome and usually happens like this to some extent. This causes me a lot of stress and anxiety, and meltdowns have resulted. And they are not pleasant!

A good (and current, at the time of writing) example of something positive is the support I have been getting from the University of Sheffield for the French degree (I am hoping to include some Spanish as well) I am doing part time. This involves communication and development where necessary. What I mean by this is that this is a learning process for me as well! For the Asperger's syndrome, we (appropriate people at the university and me) discuss what may be useful. At the moment I am meeting a student to talk in French immediately prior to the class. This is so that I can help get focused for the class, and, mostly, to help me improve at processing the information (i.e. communicating in the target language) in real time or as close to it as possible. In 2013, I found out that I have severe arthritis in my right hip. As such, I have support in mobility here, particularly since my lectures take place in the evening. I am intending to continue with communicating for this as I believe this is a vital part of best practice in support!

I often find using the internet and email useful when communicating as, in theory, I can give myself time to process information, although, I do think that other forms of communication are useful in conjunction with this. I also feel that how the written material is laid out is important as this makes the difference in whether I understand what is communicated or not!

While I am happy and comfortable with my diagnosis, I strongly sense that some other people really don't know what to do when dealing with me. I suspect they try and pursue beliefs that would work for themselves, but would never work for me. In fact, this behaviour causes serious damage. Others try to be too nice. I recognise this group are trying to help, but they aren't getting it right. It's like they are trying too hard. I feel that one of the biggest problems I face is that my opinions on support are sometimes not listened to and professionals think it's their place to make suggestions. This is where things go drastically wrong. To be honest, I know me better than anyone else and if professionals saw this and started communicating in a more appropriate manner, they might start getting it right. I have found some managers are like this as well. It is as if they are taking the 'Does he take sugar?' approach and they don't realise how insulting and patronising this is. I do think efforts are being made, but it comes over badly. I suppose this could be described as a 'well-meaning do-gooder'. It is rather frustrating! Once a good method is in place, tailor-made and bespoke, I believe being included is fruitful and rewarding for all. My personal philosophy being: living with AS and working with it.

Chapter 15

Positive Experiences for Sarah (Aged 27)

Enjoying Freedom That I Never Thought I'd Have

Sarah Galley

Introduction by Dean Worton

Like so many in this collection of chapters, Sarah sets a good example to others with Asperger's syndrome (AS). Due to criticism about their so-called shortcomings, too many people with AS just stay at home and depend heavily on their families. Sarah did not find it easy but she has self-belief and determination in spades, and despite various obstacles managed to live alone and cook for herself, and she persevered with learning to drive, getting there in the end.

Sarah is now a more independent person, and how wonderful to be able to just drive to the countryside when she wants to get away from it all. I think people with AS (and in general) should go to the countryside as often as possible, be it to drive round, walk over mountain tops, learn Nordic walking (great for people with AS), cycle into it or just get a train to a lake and sunbathe. It's a great tonic and wipes stress away. The sat-nav has made this so much more feasible for Sarah, and with similar communication technologies, getting out and about to different places and meeting new people has become so much easier, and this in turn allows people who may otherwise have been isolated to use the internet and I daresay mobile phone apps too, to connect with others in a similar situation, providing that personal safety rules are always followed.

I have had a lot of positive experiences in my life time but I would like to talk about a few of the bigger ones that have happened to me.

Flying the nest

In spring 2013 I took a decision that can be very hard for an autistic adult: I moved out to a flat just behind my parents' house. I wanted to try living on my own because I wanted my own space and I felt that could be better achieved by having my own place. It took several weeks to get all the required things for the flat as I was starting with hardly anything. However, I managed to get some second-hand furniture from a family friend which was good as it made it much more affordable. I basically ended up with things for a starter home for next to nothing, knowing that I could replace them in time if I really wanted to.

The idea of moving out was given to me when I was around the age of 21, but I felt I was not ready to go because I had not passed my driving test. Ultimately it had to be somewhere that had a parking space because then I would be able to go freely and quickly with my car to my parents' house. I always stayed at theirs at the weekend as it got lonely at times, although I had made friends with the dogs next door. In the end I'd passed my driving test by the time I moved out. That was crucial because I would not have done many of the things I have done in the past few years if I had not passed.

One of the main benefits of living on my own was that I could eat when I like and whatever I wanted. I taught myself to cook a bunch of new things and I was so chuffed with myself. I would not have survived if I had not done that as I would have been eating microwave meals or other food that was bad for me. I made vegetarian risotto the most as it is so easy to do and you can add virtually anything to it. I made several varieties and even made it with noodles, so Mum named it 'noosotto'! I'm not vegetarian but I thought that was a good place to start. I find one pot meals easier to do as I do not have to juggle with lots of pots and pans! I mostly like cooking chicken biryani, as it is so easy.

Unfortunately, I moved back home again after a year away, as things weren't always easy for me to deal with. However, being on my own helped me to understand more of what needs to happen when running a home. I feel I learned some valuable things so I can move out again at a later date. I had a lady come in each week when I lived in the flat, to check on me and make phone calls or just chat if I needed. Of course things went wrong at times, but that's part of the fun and learning process. Now, moving forward, it's up to me to keep my skills current and build on the areas I need to or maybe learn new things if I so choose!

Driving

I passed my driving test in early 2011 after my seventh go – Every time I failed I would tell my parents to sell the car and that I thought I would never do it. I was always ever so close when I did not pass. I am so happy that I did pass because it has opened up a whole new level of living and I am able to go out when I like and not rely on public transport, which can be absolutely horrendous. I do still occasionally use the bus if I feel I do not want to drive or if the place is too busy that I am going to.

I knew that I wanted to eventually drive because I have clubs that I belong to. I am in the Girl Guides and I drive to meetings each week, I am also in a disability group that is 15 miles away so it was essential for me to have that skill. Sometimes I enjoy a drive out in the countryside just to 'get lost' for a few hours, but I always have my iPad with maps on it so I know the way home if I really do get into a panic about where I am. My iPad has become my companion in the car. It's my sat-nav and my personal assistant and I would definitely be lost if I did not have it with me on a journey out!

When I get in the car I feel relaxed and in a happy place knowing I can go places, and it has meant that I can do my volunteering and be taxi to my dad when he needs a lift up to the pub! I feel so proud turning up at places in my car because, although I know it took me a little longer than most people to master, I know it's a skill I will never ever lose!

Chapter 16

How Our Negative Experiences Can Raise Awareness of Autism and Produce Positive Results for Society

A. Nonny Mouse

Introduction by Dean Worton

This is a clear case where it became necessary for the autistic individual to point out in a calm and rational way to an understanding person just how someone else's way of treating her made her feel. It should be a lesson to others on the spectrum that they should ask to be treated with the same respect as everyone else and, above all, should not put up with being treated in a particular way simply because of their condition. That A. Nonny Mouse eventually spoke out is great, and not doing so could have been detrimental for the wider autistic community. Though it should also be the case in all areas of life, an autistic adult trying for better services for autistic adults should be listened to because really who can know better than they do about what works and what doesn't? There are some autism organisations that don't recognise this and feel that only people without autism can drive things forward. I think that this view is very dangerous, and the sooner such organisations move on from that thinking the better.

What turned out to be the most positive result so far from my being autistic started out as a very negative one. I must add at this point that my take on my own, and others', autism has mostly been from a 'glass half full' perspective. I am an eternal optimist, or should I say, historically I have been thus. I have also been naive, trusting of others and bent on giving those I have helped something positive to concentrate on in their varied situations. This does not mean that I fail to appreciate that many autistic people find themselves in cruelly untenable situations on a daily basis. I simply try to help people gain a sense of perspective based in fact rather than one resulting from emotional overload promoted by comparing the current situation to others in their past that ended badly for them.

The tale I am about to relate challenged all of my previously held beliefs and shows how the opinion of others we trust can lead us to make erroneous judgements of others' motives and understanding in any given situation. It also shows that given the right support and understanding *at the right time*, the autistic person can make a positive contribution to society whilst improving their understanding of systems of which they have little or no previous knowledge.

In 2010, I became involved in the meetings leading to the setting up of my local Autism Partnership Board and, once the board was established, volunteered to be its co-chair alongside the local services autism rep. Things went okay for a time but, one day, I became overloaded when I turned up for a meeting with my co-chair. Through miscommunication and misunderstandings on both sides I was left with, as I saw it, no alternative but to resign.

My work colleague at the time, also autistic, saw the incident as proof of what he had suspected always. Namely, that autistic and non-autistic people (in this instance service personnel) were incapable of working together to effect change without the autistic partner suffering an unacceptable amount of damage and frustration.

I took this to heart and refused all contact with the board and my former colleagues on the premise that they did not understand my motives or the damage 'they' had caused me.

At this stage, I was approached by a board member who understood what had happened and suggested we meet up. This was arranged and he visited my workplace for a meeting with my colleague and me. Imagine my surprise when my colleague proceeded to tell this person that the experience had scarred me to the extent that I was now a different person! Listening to this made me realise he, too, had misinterpreted my feelings on the subject.

Thankfully, my visitor then asked me a question, 'What do you want to do about the situation and how can I help you to do it?', which cleared my confusion and gave me a means of repairing the situation.

As a result, I requested a meeting with my co-chair so that we could clear up our misunderstanding and, true to his word, the board member arranged this for us. After a two-hour meeting we were better able to see each other's point of view on the incident. Apologies were given on both sides and I returned to the board.

We both learned a lot from that encounter, which led to better practice on the board and better understanding of autistic thinking on his part, and better understanding of processes and thinking in services on mine.

This has given us a firm foundation on which to build a better way of working together to achieve mutually beneficial results for the delivery of the autism strategy. The way our board is run encourages cooperation and transparency.

Of course, it is early days but we are already seeing the benefits resulting from working together with all our members to achieve desired outcomes in an often less than autism-friendly society.

As I said at the start, this experience looked entirely negative initially, but I think without it we would not have achieved the kind of understanding or the format we have that encourages new and radical thinking instead of adherence to the historical actions and thinking that from both spheres promoted the autism spectrum/neurotypical divide that is so unhelpful to overcoming barriers to cooperation.

Chapter 17

Aspies' Experiences in Theatre

C.A. Smart

Introduction by Dean Worton

There is an over-riding theme in the *Insider Intelligence* series of books of recommending certain activities to help people with Asperger's syndrome (AS) to lead happier lives, and theatre is another one to add into the mix. AS is synonymous with serious thinking, but Fooling sounds like a great way to let oneself go and have fun, and theatre in general could aid social confidence. I appreciate that for some people with AS, there could be an overpowering social atmosphere especially where there are issues with physical contact. Where this is the case, writing plays to be acted by others could also be a great outlet. Having a monologue that you have written acted on the other side of the world is certainly something to be proud of. C.A. Smart has had a lot to deal with over the years and after a lot of self-criticism it's great that she no longer feels that anyone is letting her down.

I would strongly recommend that anyone with AS embraces comedy and humour where possible. Five to ten minutes of comedy every morning and just before bed, be it recorded or on a video streaming internet site like YouTube, would be a great way to start and end the day in a better mood. It won't necessarily stop depression, but it could be a step in the right direction. Laughter releases lots of endorphins, which is a very healthy thing.

I am a 41-year-old woman, diagnosed with Asperger's syndrome four years ago. I was also diagnosed with paranoid schizophrenia aged 17. I want to talk about positive experiences to do with theatre, specifically drama workshops, studying and writing for theatre, and the role theatre has had so far in my life in the context of my diagnosis with Asperger's.

Looking back at my childhood, I can now identify specific difficulties related to Asperger's – for example, with playground situations, or not being able to take part in imaginative play with toys and other children, playing alone a lot. I was always acting or dancing by myself and with anyone I could drag into my performances. I devised short plays for my siblings quite frequently. As opposed to other forms of play, I was able to write, act in and direct my own creations. My parents sent me on week-long summer camps with a specific emphasis on drama where I learned not to overact and realised how much I loved the theatre.

I took drama throughout school, but during my A levels it became impossible to succeed because of an emerging psychosis. This psychosis lasted for many months and after becoming well again I found myself capable of less than before. The struggle to get truly better is a long one after each episode of psychosis. Unable to work, I started volunteering for a few hours a week.

After not thinking about the theatre very much for many years, I met someone who had participated in a Fooling workshop (a form of comedy improvisation, exploring the archetype of the Fool). The company held one- and two-week residential workshops in the UK and on the continent. My first one was held in the middle of nowhere in the hills surrounding Sienna. I also went to Hannover, Trier and Cornwall. There were workshops all day, learning about the idea of the Fool and how to let go of our fears and perform in 'The Empty Space'. I really enjoyed my time with the groups but remember experiencing a number of specific difficulties that I now associate with being Asperger's. I found meal times very tough with all the small talk, and the contact dance was impossible for me. I had to stop my involvement with the group, not understanding how to deal with these issues.

In 2007 I met and later married someone with Asperger's. Neither of us knew we were 'Aspies' ourselves at the time we met. Our understanding of each other has taken away difficulties that would otherwise have been insurmountable. It is not always easy to identify our respective quirks and it can be frustrating. At least we now know why and we can deal positively with it. Having had so many psychotic breaks over the years, it has now become inevitable to think of myself as disabled. I have had a long period of being well and am slightly better adjusted.

In January 2013 I found myself investigating community theatre, and short courses. I was lucky to find a writing mentor who works with a disability theatre.

My diagnosis of Asperger's has given me the knowledge and the courage to fight through the difficulties I still experience socially. I don't expect other people to understand what is happening to me, but I can at least forgive myself and put everything into perspective.

Two years ago, I went to a theatre group for the 'socially excluded'. We played drama games and performed short improvisations and movement pieces for each other. I am now less self-stigmatising and also, non-judgemental about other people who also have difficulties. In the meantime I have written six short monologues, three ten-minute plays and a radio play.

One of my short monologues was performed in Connecticut, and I had a professional rehearsed reading with the theatre I am working with. Another of my short plays was showcased in Shawnee on Delaware, shortlisted for full production.

I have participated in playwriting courses with a local theatre, which has led to my first production at a showcase event for new writers, 'Platform 15' at the Theatre Royal Plymouth in The Drum. I have recently had this play published by Lazy Bee Scripts.

In the run up to Christmas last year I co-wrote for a devised theatre company, 'The Lab Company 2014', at the Theatre Royal Plymouth – a supported group for early career professionals. This experience in particular has given me the confidence to self-produce my full-length play, which I have been writing for the past two years. The enthusiasm other people have for my writing is infectious, it makes me want to write more.

I have since written a short monologue, 'Insider', about a woman who turns into a spider. It has been shown at two 'Scratch Nights', one at The Rose Playhouse, Bankside, London, and one at The Royal William Yard, Plymouth with 'BETA Scratch Nights'.

I am now producing this monologue and a short related piece by a good actor friend from the 'Stepping Out Theatre Company', taking both to the Edinburgh Fringe Festival for eight performances in August.

As part of the writing process I have held a 'table read', a 'rehearsed read through' and a 'scripted read through' with an invited audience, with local actors and a young director for my full-length play. This has helped me to see what works and what doesn't. These are amazing experiences, hearing my work out loud and liked by other people. Without the actors', other writers' and my family's enthusiasm I might not still be doing this.

We are now a limited company, Coffee House Theatre Company, with a website. We have begun to raise funds for a tour of regional MIND Centres and a full production at the Barbican Theatre, Plymouth, probably in the early part of 2017.

Since being diagnosed, I am more compassionate with myself. Having had schizophrenia as well, there have been many hopes dashed by psychotic breaks. Knowing I have Asperger's gives me a lot of comfort. Rather than being afraid, I now expect the difficulties I have and do not have to condemn myself for my failings. I am more understanding of my husband's idiosyncracies and have more joy in life generally. I am able to acknowledge myself more. I know the difficulties I am going to encounter and have the courage to face people without my previous hang-ups. I feel on a more even footing with the rest of humanity. Previously, I found myself to be unusual, even amongst other schizophrenics. Realising at this age that my difficulties had a reason in the domain of Asperger's gives me more courage now than ever before. I can do what I need to do, meeting actors and directors, being in a large group, exposing myself quite profoundly to criticism and directions and suggestions. It doesn't feel anymore as if anyone is putting me down, and I no longer have to think, 'Sod this, I'm no good, I am going to give up and do something else.'

Chapter 18

The Day I (Nearly)
Became a Male Prostitute

Atul Movelis

Introduction by Dean Worton

What I find so refreshing about this chapter is the way that Atul just puts his ordeal down to being another life experience. I'm quite sure that when the main story unfolded for real he would have undergone several emotions of fear, terror and distress, and it is certainly not a scenario I would like to see anyone with autism or otherwise to ever have to endure. But Atul clearly lives in the now. It is not happening now and the fact that he has moved on and puts it down to experience shows brilliant stoicism, which is often a good trait of Asperger's syndrome (AS).

Needless to say, this story should be a warning to others to be careful with money and other people, especially where foreign travel is involved, but I truly admire the way that Atul isn't upset by his teenage naivety and instead is able to laugh at himself and be fascinated by autistic behaviour. All too often the positive traits of AS are hidden away and not celebrated, so the person with AS is not always aware that they have so much going for them. Atul seems to have a well-developed sense of humour and to feel

lucky to be on the spectrum and to really embrace
the positive traits.

Ah, the naivety of the wonderful nature of autism! To think
that an apparently intelligent man (with a few degrees
and the like) could still fall into such an obvious trap as to
agree to be a male prostitute without realising it – what a
wonderful and intriguing population the autistic one is! So,
to set the scene...

Our hero is in India. He has absolutely no understanding
of money – if he has it, it gets spent. If he doesn't have it,
he assumes that something will occur that will sort him
out. This has been a recurring problem – for example, at
university he happily spends hundreds of pounds buying so-
called 'friends' drinks and food of an evening, only to realise
the next day that funds have been depleted (and it's only the
first week of term). Oddly, to him, these 'friends' no longer
associate with him! He has assumed (very, very wrongly)
that such favours would be returned; sadly, it seems that
his sense of fair play does not appear to be as widely shared
as he had thought. Incidentally, to this day he still finds
himself astonished at the lack of fairness in the world, and
continues to make naive judgements and is constantly let
down. He refuses, of course, to change his stance – that
everyone should be given the chance to be trusted prior to
them proving him wrong, which they usually do. He remains
mystified by this, but is eternally optimistic that one day the
world will wake up, whack itself on the arse, and exclaim,
'We have been getting it all wrong! Let's stop telling those
naughty fibs, let's be fair, honest and equitable, treat all
people with fairness and respect, and get along'; until that
day, he has learned that he is likely to be sorely disappointed
(often daily) when his expectations of social justice and
fairness are mysteriously blindsided.

Back to India! It is the night before he flies home. He is – literally – penniless (or, technically, rupee-less). Not a problem; lots of people in India live on the streets and go hungry, why should he be any different? The trouble is, our hero is somewhat disorganised. He tends to live in the moment, on a day-by-day basis. Rarely does this fine chap think beyond the here and now when it comes to his own life; interestingly (possibly) he is often found to be giving detailed advice to others about the inter-connectivity of actions and consequences; sometimes, it appears, the advice is unwelcome.

So, the day before flying he looks for his passport and flight details only to discover that there is an airport tax to get out of the country. He does not have this. What to do? (The latter is a rhetorical question; any clever answers you may have are long overdue, but my thanks if you have thought of any; shame you weren't there with me to help me out way back then!)

He wanders the streets, mulling things over. He does not have much in the way of things to sell, but he does have his portable music player. He loves his music, does our hero, and feels very insecure when it is unavailable to him. He needs to listen to specific songs before sleep. Sometimes, he needs to listen to specific parts of tracks numerous times (with the appropriate integer, dependent on circumstances, of course), so that the world is 'just right'. He knows that there is no real logical explanation for this, but accepts that it works really rather well for him, and is something that he cultivates to keep him more or less sane in a bewildering world. He doesn't mind the world being bewildering (having long since made the entirely incorrect assumption that it was bewildering to all); what he really does mind, though, is people telling him not to do the things that make it bearable for him. Just because most people (oddly) don't like listening to a particular snippet of a particular track a particular set number of times, surely doesn't mean that he shouldn't, and he reacts not so well when told otherwise – he's not harming anyone else, and he sure is doing himself a whole lot of good. However, on reflection, he decides that not having access to music for 24 hours or so is probably better than unlawfully becoming a homeless person on the streets of Mumbai, so decides to try and sell his gear. He goes from hotel reception to hotel reception, asking anyone he can find if they want to buy his music player. A miracle occurs! A very friendly gentleman overhears the discourse, and approaches our hero: 'Do you need money? I can lend you some!' Unbelievable. What a stroke of chance! The friendly gentleman helpfully explains further, 'I will give you x amount of rupees – half now, and half in the morning. You can stay in my hotel room.' What a result! What a lovely chap! Not only does our hero get the funds to leave the country, he also has a comfy bed to stay in! The friendly gentleman keeps banging on about how having twin beds is not a problem, as he can push them together to make a double – this strikes our hero as a rather odd comment to keep making, but people so often make odd remarks that he has learnt simply to smile, agree and mentally set aside some time in his brain for later on to muse on what on Earth people are on about. This is a strategy he has used so often that it is almost second nature. His brain spends quite some time mulling over what people have said on a day-to-day basis, and trying – usually unsuccessfully – to work out what they meant. So, this is a common experience and one that does not seem out of the ordinary in any way.

Something that does strikes him as singularly odd – the friendly gentleman seems reluctant to give his name and address, which our hero insists on having so that he can reimburse the money. He refuses to accept the money as a 'gift', which was the offer, as there is no discernible reason why a stranger should offer a financial gift, and he would prefer to agree clear loan terms. Eventually, the friendly gentleman tells our hero that he will give him a name and address in the hotel bedroom, and off they set.

Ten minutes or so later, the friendly gentleman has given our hero some cash, drawn the curtains (this is strange, it's only afternoon and still light – why is he closing the curtains?), pushed the twin beds together (brain – where are you, why is he doing this?), locked the door and has started to undress. Aha! Epiphany! Brain finally puts the clues together, and it dawns on our hero that the friendly gentleman might not be being friendly just for the sake of being friendly, and that there may be expectations involved otherwise hitherto unconsidered. After hasty consideration, brain concludes that said expectations are not agreeable, and that it – alongside its physical companion, the body – would rather like to no longer be there. BUT! What is a socially acceptable way of excusing one's self from a (semi) pre-paid sexual encounter? Our hero has long since accepted that he struggles with what is socially accepted in everyday life, so to try and work out what to do in this situation is likely to be far too neurologically complex, and poor brain is beginning to implode. Luckily, brain is just lively enough to tell mouth to ask the (perhaps not so) friendly gentleman if he can just nip out to inform his friends where he is staying for the night. He detests lying (not only is he categorically not telling anyone anything, but he doesn't even have any friends to tell!), but sees no other immediate solution. As he leaves the hotel he has overwhelming feelings of guilt – for taking the money without providing services, for having inadvertently misled the (perhaps not so) friendly gentleman and for having to tell a lie. He also realises, much to his dismay, that he never did get a name and address, so while he managed to get safely home, he never could return the 'loan'. This troubles him to this day. In fact, he has to add this to the growing list of 'things that cannot be resolved' that brain has to cope with, poor thing.

So, you may be wondering why this has been chosen as a 'positive experience'. Well, for starters it makes for a fun anecdote when I am unsure of what to say on social occasions – though, sadly, this strategy does not always work, depending on who is present. To be fair, I find that the best way of coping with social situations (parties, and the like) is simply to avoid them! It can be so terrifying when faced with people and there being a requirement for that thing that is called 'chit chat'; I mean, please, what is that all about? How splendid would it be if it were 'allowed' to be social by attendance only, i.e. physical presence, and then quietly, causing no fuss, read a Kindle (other devices are available)? I've gone all gooey just thinking about it...autism Nirvana (in the Buddhist context, not the band, though, on reflection, I wonder what an autism-related Novoselic/Cobain, with side order of Grohl, experience might look like? However, I feel that I am in danger of digressing...).

Anyway, my main reason for choosing it is that, actually, it delights me to think of just how fabulously interesting the autistic person can be (I don't specifically mean me, by the way; I am dull as dishwater – though, if your dishwater is dull prior to using it you probably need to empty the sink/receptacle and use fresh water instead). So full of contradictions, so full of mystery, so full of surprises! What would the world be like without such fascinating characters? The autistic population undoubtedly adds to the rich depth of humanity in intriguing, beguiling and compelling ways – and, surely, that is a positive?

It fascinates me how extreme the diversity is between different types of intelligence. Academic intelligence, social intelligence, common sense intelligence – there can be such a huge disparity between them in the autistic brain, with examples of brilliance in some areas and, let's face it, complete ineptitude in others. The day I nearly became a male prostitute remains firmly embedded in my memory. I have a pretty good memory for some events, while others seem to disappear from memory straight away – I don't know why. I can recall exact visual images and verbal exchanges in some circumstances, usually in explicit detail, but often forget if I have actually said something to someone, or just thought about it. I often (well, almost always, actually) rehearse conversations – sometimes several times, sometimes hours in advance – and on occasion these imaginary conversations become real to me, and I subsequently become convinced that I have had them. I have to ask people, 'Did we have a conversation about...?' – at which point I frequently get 'that look' – you know the one, the 'has he gone a bit bonkers again' look. Again, this is something to be cheerful about – the ability to laugh at one's self is something that I have learned, and to great effect. It is too easy as an autistic person to become embittered about the ways of the world – and, to be fair, it sometimes isn't all that easy to be autistic in this world – but developing the ability to take the difficult times and reflect on them with a certain sense of humour can help lift the spirits somewhat.

Having a good understanding of why one makes such a fool of one's self can also be liberating. To acknowledge that it is the nature of one's brain, rather than something ascribed to a personality defect can be a great relief. It doesn't stop me making a fool of myself, but it does help me to not blame myself constantly and, at the same time, helps me to not blame the people laughing at me! This does not excuse behaviour: I believe that we are all accountable for our own behaviour, but if that then leads to a problem – if I have (inadvertently) upset someone – should I blame myself, if I genuinely believe that it is the way in which autism affects me that has led to the problem? Well, no – I shouldn't. BUT – it is subsequently my responsibility to try and learn from that mistake and do my best to reduce any risk of it recurring. Otherwise I would be morally in the wrong. I truly believe that being morally in the right, and working towards that goal each and every day, is something that most people with autism strive for. Sadly, I also believe that when we do 'get it wrong' we are often made to feel so terrible about it that we shoulder all the guilt, sometimes to crippling effect. Strangely, when we 'get it right' there seems to be little in the way of praise...

Humour is supposedly something that autistic people lack – so it states in some of the literature, anyway. I can categorically correct that view, which is, in fact, a nonsense: we may have a rather different sense of humour, but the ability to laugh – and laugh at ourselves, often – is something that we should all hold precious, autistic or not. Many autistic people have a fabulous sense of humour, as well as a sublime sense of endearing and gentle self-deprecation, which can be a suitable companion throughout life. I don't doubt that autistic people do face real trauma in life – as can anyone – quite unlike my own experience outlined above. But those times when we make a social gaffe, when we appear to be the idiot, where we find ourselves the laughing stock, shouldn't be taken to heart! Learn, then laugh. And those of you who are laughing *at* us and not *with* us – perhaps you should be looking more at your own moral codes, instead of questioning ours.

Do I consider myself vulnerable? Yes, absolutely. Do I consider myself to be defective in some way? Not in the least. Am I inept in many areas of life compared to other non-autistic people of similar intellectual abilities? Oh, yes. Do I consider myself as somehow less than them? Not in the slightest. Do I find it hilarious that I once nearly became a male prostitute without realising? Absolutely! After all, life wouldn't be half as interesting without such things occurring, would it?

Chapter 19

My Radio Show

Making People Happier with My Strong Music Interest and Knowledge

Gerard Wilkie

Introduction by Dean Worton

It is great how much of a positive thing Gerard has made out of his passion for music. Some of the instruments he plays sound fun and a great way for anyone with Asperger's syndrome (AS) to let off steam. What is so wonderful about his story is not only how much he is able to share his passion, but that so many people put their Friday evenings into his hands as he plays music for them, and how he can nearly always find a requested track or suitable alternative and make a dull hospital stay where enjoyment is in short supply that bit more bearable by brightening up their day. This explodes the myth that people with AS don't care about others; he enjoys making people happy! Being asked to control the programmes and train the presenters shows how appreciated Gerard is. Whilst all this is going on, you would probably never know that this man has AS.

I am a 45-year-old male with Asperger's, and have a deep interest in music. I am very happily married, with two children and they are all fully aware of the time I devote to my hobby – I play the mandolin, flute, fiddle, ukulele, didgeridoo and countless other musical instruments, and when not playing an instrument I can usually be found with my headphones on, listening to music. I enjoy most styles of music.

I have turned my hobby into an interesting positive experience for myself in that for the past eight years I have been volunteering for my local hospital radio station, Radio Grapevine, which is based in St John's Hospital, Livingston, West Lothian.

I started off as a request collector, where I was going around the wards meeting patients and asking them if they wanted us to play a request for them on air. I particularly enjoyed the knowledge that, if I managed to get a request played for somebody, this would greatly help to brighten up their day and hopefully give them a positive experience of staying in hospital. I have an encyclopedic knowledge of music, so if we didn't have the particular song that the patient requested available in the studio I would always be able to find a suitable alternative for them. Additionally, I know the studio inside out as well as what tunes we have and don't have, so I was always able to put my hands on a request quickly.

After several months request collecting, I was promoted to be presenter of my own show, which to start with was a request show in which I played the requests we had received from patients. I presented the request show for seven years and now present a feature show on Friday nights, the Folk Den, in which I delve into my particular musical love, folk music. I was brought up in a musical family, and Mother spent time as a folk music promoter and organised a regular folk club here in Scotland back in the 1960s and 1970s. In my show I try to draw on all the old tunes and artists I remember when growing up, so it tends to include a lot of music by the likes of the Dubliners and Steeleye Span, but I try to play as much current folk music as I can.

Presenting the Folk Den is another deeply positive experience for me, as I am drawing on a deep personal interest of which I have a great knowledge, and I know that there are people out there listening to what I do, and again, most importantly, hopefully they are enjoying what I do – and that is what drives me to work so hard at preparing my show.

We now stream online, which means that it is not only patients within the hospital who can listen to us, but anyone anywhere in the world can listen to us online. I really like the idea that I can share my deep personal interest in music and the positive experiences that broadcasting it to an audience potentially around the world has given me, and so work hard at preparing my show and striving to be as professional in what I do as I can be, bearing in my mind that what I do is voluntary and is done after my day job.

I joined Radio Grapevine's management committee three years ago, first in the role of secretary, where I took the notes for all of the committee meetings, and fielded queries from outside bodies, but now I am the station's programme controller, which means that I am responsible for the station's sound and output, and for training people to become presenters. I am loving this role, as it gives me the opportunity and excuse to spend all my time listening to music and choosing songs and shows that we can broadcast on air. Bearing in mind that it is primarily a hospital radio show, I feel I know which songs work and which don't, so I try to ensure that we play appropriate songs.

We take our music out to the wider community by attending roadshows. This is an important aspect of volunteering at hospital radio, as the income generated provides us with a valuable source of income, without which we would be unable to function. I enjoy doing the roadshows, particularly setting up the equipment and playing the music to the audience, but sometimes my Asperger's makes me feel outside my comfort zone if I am the presenter. I try my hardest nevertheless, but my Asperger's never puts me off enjoying the events. I am at my happiest when I am alone in the studio, talking to an 'unseen' audience – in that type of situation I can really be myself, but when in front of people I can freeze up a little bit. Still, I suppose that is to be expected, but as I have previously mentioned, my enjoyment of taking part always makes it a positive experience for me.

I consider myself very lucky to be an autistic adult who has managed to find a way of volunteering that shares my deep personal interests and provides entertainment to the wider community. I look forward to all the time I spend in hospital radio, more than I do in going out to my day job – and to be perfectly honest, if I didn't enjoy it I wouldn't do it. I have found that it is an area in which I am able to draw on all my strengths and feel very proud of what I have achieved.

Chapter 20

Turning Points

*How Thinking Outside the Box
Helped Me Overcome Hurdles
in My Music Teaching Career*

Eloise B.

Introduction by Dean Worton

This has some parallels with the story of A. Nonny Mouse in that Eloise's positive experience stems from something that started off as rather negative. Teaching can be a very rewarding career for people on the spectrum and I know a few people with Asperger's syndrome (AS) who teach. The teachers with AS that I know do tend to teach either in adult education, or more specialist subjects individually, or in small groups, usually to people with specific interests outside of daytime mainstream teaching. Perhaps this works better than mainstream schools, which can be a hostile environment for some people with AS to deal with.

I'm sure that this is not always the case and I am sure that there are many successful mainstream teachers with AS, but with lack of support it seems that it could unfortunately end quite brutally. However, good fortune can come from the most unlikely of sources, and if a person with AS receives enough criticism, it is not surprising that they would fear the worst so can be thoroughly stunned when the opposite occurs. Eloise's experience is proof that you can never guarantee something ending badly if the outcome has yet to be revealed. Just await the result and you never know your luck.

This is my positive experience; but positives can sometimes emerge from the most difficult of circumstances, so first I must revisit one of the worst times of my life.

I sat on the train staring glumly out of the window. I could think of many places I would rather be, almost anywhere in fact. I felt nauseous with anxiety and my mind raced at 100 miles per hour round and round the same tiny track. At that time I had no idea who I really was. The only solution to my weird life my mind could come up with was that I was a freak, an alien, a person everyone hated, and that this shameful secret must be hidden at all costs. I had paid the price for this unhealthy situation with repeated episodes of anxiety and depression throughout my adult life and now I was on my way to a situation that was putting extreme pressure on me. I was dreading it.

I was in the middle of a PGCE course or Postgraduate Certificate in Education. I had been teaching musical instruments for about ten years and had managed to scrape a living, but London was an expensive place to live. I felt that I was stuck in a rut. If I couldn't improve my salary, I would continue my precarious existence in rented accommodation for the foreseeable future. The route to a better paid and more secure job seemed to be through the PGCE. This was a class teaching qualification, whereas I was teaching small groups or individuals, but that seemed to be irrelevant. The qualification was all that mattered.

When the possibility of doing the PGCE course had first arisen I had dismissed it immediately as something I simply could not do. I assumed that the interpersonal and social skills required would be way beyond me, but somehow I had been persuaded that everything would fall into place. They were going to train me. Somehow the miracle would happen and I would be transformed into a sociable and articulate being – I knew nothing of Asperger's at the time.

I remember when I first started to teach musical instruments. It felt so strange to have to talk; not just a muttered response to someone else's initiative, but taking the lead and speaking fluently. As I was talking mostly about music I gradually managed to expand my vocal delivery into something like a suitable style, but even at that time, through the fog of my misperceptions about myself and the world in general, I was aware of shortcomings. It was clearly a requirement to offer pupils praise and encouragement, but how could I do that? Most of what they were doing was not particularly special and it would be extremely rare for me to be genuinely delighted by their efforts. So this meant in effect lying and pretending, something that was incredibly difficult for me. It was also hard for me to make eye contact during the lessons; instead I would stare intently at the piece of music as if it held all the answers and only make the briefest of glances towards my pupil. At the beginning or end of the lesson while the pupil was getting out or putting away their instrument there was a rather uncomfortable silence. I would always greet them and ask how they were, but was then at a loss for anything else to say until we got on with the music.

Finally in my forties I had decided to embark on the PGCE course. I had already visited two schools, which had not been particularly satisfactory. The first had been a good school, but music was not a priority there and the department was rather run down. It worried me that aspects of the training did not happen in the methodical way detailed (very detailed!) in the course guide. I can see now that this would always be unlikely to happen in a busy school, but at the time I was convinced that I was missing out.

The second school was strange. I can't provide details here for reasons of confidentiality, but things were very far from right in the school and in the department. I was left on my own most of the time without the necessary skills and experience to cope and predictably ended up having a week off with stress, though I think I pretended it was something else at the time. The next time, my tutor assured me, things would be much better. She had previous experience of the school I was to attend, and she was sure I would get on wel there.

So here I was on my way to the third and final school placement for the PGCE course; ten weeks of teaching class music to 11–18-year-olds. I assumed at this point that I would pass the course. Received wisdom was that anyone who was likely to fail would have been weeded out by this point and only successful candidates were left. I was about to prove this theory wrong.

First there was my mentor, the head of music at the school. I can see now that she was a bully. She was the type of teacher children hate, but are so scared of they simply do not dare to misbehave. When I first met her I explained that I had had some difficulties at the previous school and might need some extra support. This was of course like the proverbial red rag to the bull. She wanted a student primarily to take some of her classes, which would free up her time for support work with the GCSE students. An ineffectual, anxious wimp who needed 'extra help' was no use to her. I think that she instantly dismissed me as a hopeless case.

The music lessons themselves were exhausting. There was often a high level of noise as children attempted to play instruments, and constant demands on my attention as I tried to manage the large class and deal with behaviour issues. I needed a lot of recovery time in a private space somewhere, but I didn't get it. The lessons continued relentlessly and there were people everywhere. Even when I had some spare time to tackle the massive amount of coursework, I couldn't concentrate because my mind was still in a state of frantic over-arousal from the lessons.

Things were not going well with the music department either. I hadn't received any of the written observations I needed and my meetings with my mentor to discuss my progress were cursory or non-existent. The worst moment was probably when the teachers from the department and the other student teacher went for a pub lunch, but didn't invite me. I hated it but at least the end was in sight; I was counting down the days.

The end of the placement was approaching and my anxiety levels were stratospheric. I had completely overloaded and the slightest provocation would send me crashing down. My tutor arrived for her final visit and I was expecting that this would finally release me from the torture, but it was not to be. Suddenly she was saying that she wasn't happy, that I needed more time to become more confident. I was to spend two more weeks in the school and was to have special meetings and observations with the deputy head.

I became frantic; there was no way I could spend two more weeks in the school. It would drive me insane, but if I left I would throw away all the work that I had done up to this point. I continued, but the comments of my tutor had destroyed me. I was going to fail. The end, when it came, was at least partly on my own terms. My tutor arranged for the director of the PGCE course to come to do my final observation, which was arranged for one of the most difficult classes in the school. The lesson was a disaster and at the end I walked up to the director, said 'Okay, I know I've failed' and walked out of the school without waiting to hear any of their comments. I went home and collapsed.

I am well aware that so far this has been far from a positive experience, but bear with me as things are about to improve. I was at home with no job and very little money, scanning advertisements for future prospects when the PGCE director phoned. He told me that if I ever wanted to redo the final placement in the future he would ensure that I had a place as long as he was in charge of the course. At that time it was the last thing I felt like doing, but something made me keep my options open and I thanked him and agreed. Shortly after this I saw an advert for a job teaching instruments in the north of England. I applied, went for interview and got the job.

A couple of years later I was beginning to settle down in my new home and job and the idea of the PGCE began to enter my mind again. The horror of the previous experience was still fresh in my mind, but I was being paid less than colleagues who had a PGCE for doing the same job, which seemed so unfair. I did some research and found that it was now possible to do some of the teaching practice as instrumental teaching thereby reducing the amount of class teaching I would need to do. I could also find my own school and mentor so I could make sure that it would be someone who would give me the necessary support. It was an extremely difficult decision to make as the previous experience had left considerable mental scars, but I finally decided to go for it. I asked for support from my employer and re-applied for the PGCE.

The school I was to visit this time was in a small post-industrial town and in a much less affluent area. The atmosphere at the school, though, was friendly and supportive, and the behaviour was much better. I had already been working at this school for a while teaching instruments so knew what to expect. Before the placement started I made perhaps the single most important decision. I went to my GP and asked for medication to control the excessive anxiety that I knew I would feel. I am fortunate in that this type of medication works well for me. After I had explained the situation, the GP agreed to prescribe for me while I was doing the course.[1]

I kept chanting 'calm, calm' like a mantra to myself as I began the final teaching practice for the second time. This time the teacher who was to be my mentor, whom I'll call Jan, was incredibly supportive. At first she intervened when children misbehaved and dealt with the troublemakers herself. This went against the approved wisdom that intervening undermines the student teacher, but the children realised that they weren't going to get away with anything and for me it was perfect. All I had to do was copy what Jan had done to control the class, as she gradually began to reduce her role in my lessons. Copying people was fine. I had been doing that all my life so was something of an expert by this stage. I also found some useful books on behaviour management, especially those by Bill Rogers.[2] I realised that teaching was in fact not the same as general socialising at all. There were lists of instructions with bullet points:

- do this

- then do this

- finally do this.

I tried some of these instructions word for word and to my amazement they worked. It seemed that teaching was a skill that you could learn methodically; it wasn't just something that people did because they were good at socialising or naturally outward going.

---

1   Editors' note: medication might be effective for some people with excessive anxiety but needs to be carefully considered and only in consultation with a trained medical professional.

2   Bill Rogers taught for many years before becoming an education consultant and author. His most popular book is *Classroom Behaviour*, 4th Edition (2015) published by Sage Publications.

Jan's approach to supporting me was beginning to work. I actually started to gain some confidence. Observations were coming in really positive with just the right level of constructive criticism. I was only in the school three days a week because of the instrumental teaching element so I had the opportunity to get away from the relentless slog of class teaching and back to familiar activities. Things seemed to be going my way this time.

As time went on I began to realise that teaching was much more closely related to performing than to socialising. I had been performing on musical instruments from an early age through to music college and playing professionally in London. I loved performing music and it came naturally to me. Teaching is not a reciprocal activity like socialising. You are standing in front of a class and entertaining them, especially in music lessons. A different element of my character began to come to the fore as I started to transfer my performing skills to the classroom arena using the voice and body instead of my instrument. I became a better actor.

The teaching practice was drawing to a close and everyone seemed to be happy. There was just one final hurdle to overcome. The headteacher of the school was to visit to do my final observation. The advantage of this was that the pupils would tend to behave well as they were scared of the head, but I wondered what would happen if he wasn't happy. Could everything go wrong at the last moment? The lesson seemed to go reasonably well and I waited nervously for his feedback at the end.

His first reaction was surprise. He had thought that I might struggle with class teaching as I was so quiet, but this did not appear to be the case. The lesson was confident (no-one had ever called me confident before!), well-presented and I had tackled difficult pupils to try to get some work from them. His final comment rings in my ears to this day: *'You have the makings of a very fine teacher indeed.'*

It was all over finally and I had passed. The contrast with my previous attempt was stunning. Not only had I passed, but I had done well. It was a moment of immense significance in my life, because I had succeeded at something I believed I couldn't do.

Looking back now the course was also the start of a process that led eventually to another turning point in my life. A couple of years later after trying to cope with too many new activities at work, I had another major meltdown and needed time off with stress. As I was off work I had to go to the GP, who suggested counselling. In the end I saw a number of people, who all seemed to be puzzled by the descriptions I gave of my experiences. Frustrated by the lack of progress, I started my own investigations into what could be going wrong with my life and why it was so different to everyone else's. Eventually I found out about Asperger's, which felt like coming out of the fog into the bright and dazzling light of the sun for the first time ever. I finally knew who I was and perhaps even more importantly that there were others like me. I wasn't alone. Perhaps if my life had taken a different course this would never have happened.

On the practical front, the improvement in my finances and the cheaper prices in the north of England meant that I could buy a house and this in turn meant that I was allowed to keep pets. My dream of owning a dog came true and now I have a constant companion who is always glad to see me and accepts his crazy owner exactly as she is. Life has changed so much for the better.

One of the proudest moments of my life was walking across the stage at the Sage Centre in Gateshead to collect my PGCE certificate. I had rarely felt pride in any academic achievements at school, as I had a good memory for words and facts, which made learning easy in most subjects. My achievements in music were of course a source of pride for me and were in fact my sole identity for many years, but music was something that I was naturally good at. The PGCE was different. It was something that involved people and that I was therefore not naturally good at. I had to struggle so much to achieve it, coming back after a horrendous experience and trying again to succeed second time round. I had never done anything so hard in my life and it meant so much to me for that reason.

Chapter 21

Why Bother?

Aiming to Create Social
Fairness and Harmony

Maurice Frank

Introduction by Dean Worton

The following chapter might not be what you were expecting. When you think about positive experiences, you generally think in terms of happy thoughts and things that make you proud, certainly not related to dealing with strong feelings of anger. I have known Maurice for a long time and have always known him to have very strong and unique in-depth views. This is reflected in his chapter but I would ask that all readers please bear with Maurice. Whilst the beginning part of the chapter might seem anything but positive, it does take a lighter turn, showing that Maurice is a proactive individual with a very caring attitude not only towards others with Asperger's syndrome (AS) but to society as a whole.

It must be stressed that Maurice is just one individual with AS and that the strong and unique viewpoints expressed within the chapter are Maurice's own and the genuine way that he sees the world based around his own experiences as an adult growing up with AS in (for him) a harsh world. Two people with AS are as different from each other as two predominant neurotypes (PNTs) are. In places where the arguments used in the document have become particularly controversial, there will be an editors' note to point out that the views expressed belong to Maurice and are not necessarily shared by myself, Luke or the publishers. You can of course choose whether or not you agree with the points that Maurice is making.[1]

Some people do get angry when they feel that someone (including themselves) is being treated unfairly. This is fine provided that it is dealt with constructively and nobody is actually physically or mentally harmed in the process. In many ways, I think that people with AS/autism have good reason to be less than happy with the way that they and others on the spectrum are treated and the standard of service they receive. Whether or not I have always agreed with Maurice's approach, what I have always admired about him is that he stands up for himself and others, while too many other people just allow unfair practices to continue to happen involving people on the spectrum and society in general. I believe that Maurice's strong sense of justice is what makes this chapter ultimately positive, and about things that he can be justifiably proud of.

Why bother?

After injustice and trauma permanently affecting your life, where can positives be found? Many Aspies who were either not discovered, or not embraced into a helpful autism scene, until later in our lives, are affected by this question. We need

---

1   Editors' note: this chapter contains several opinions that the reader might not expect to read in a book about positive experiences. Please note that whilst they are not necessarily the opinions of the editors or publishers, they are the views of the writer.

you to appreciate that there is no glib formula for happiness that can wipe it away.

Happiness is not even my objective, in a world where anyone dies unfairly young. A moment's thought on that shows how selfish it is to be a trivial jolly character, swanning around ecstatically feeling good about everything, in a world full of heartbreaking news. How long will that unwise state last? Until it ends in the impact when a shock happens that you were not prepared for. How settled do your emotions feel then, when you suddenly lose something, or buy a bad product, or get spoken to unfairly grumpily, or distracted unfairly from the task you want to focus on? For me, all functioning and ability to focus is wrecked for the rest of the day by the jolt and I feel disorientated, in a panic of suddenly needing to reconstruct a whole coping strategy for the day.

Positivity is not then for me an entire state of mind to pursue. Indeed I have learned never to go through any day feeling jauntily confident, in order not to have too far to fall from that state. But a practical need in keeping able to function, to avoid crippling despair, is to hold onto the positivity of reasons why it is worth functioning, why you can make any progress towards any of your goals. It is clearly fairer to perceive that you can than to accept any harsh worldly wise voice stamping on your possibilities.

Start from a low base: that all progress is positive. That is a fair and common sense assertion. Constantly telling yourself to do better is just a negative feeling. It is evil how all the unending misery spread by school teachers with that attitude has taken away positivity and buried it under crushing despair.[2]

Tell yourself the positives that show that your objectives are possible, and the positives done by each step you take progressing towards them. List these to yourself all the time, in every situation. When I get thinking time at each day's end

---

2   Editors' note: this could be seen as a 'sweeping' statement and is the view of the writer and not necessarily of the editors or publishers.

I do this. It gives me an uplift of mood to sleep on. This has kept me going through over 30 years of life's upward trend, away from its lowest point in my diabolical school crisis, into asserting my identity as a libertarian, into diagnosis and into belonging to fulfilling Aspie society.

It is positive to have come so far. It all built up gradually with each step encouraged by those before it. I can bask in the victory that the disciplinarian gifted education movement of my childhood lies utterly discredited, and I am supporting the better society that discredited it whenever I work for the Aspie scene.

I had the entire normal course of my life wrecked in my early teenage years, by school homework set too intensively and ambitiously. My Aspie strength at absorbing facts about intellectual topics of interest had given me some good positive learning experiences in the freedom of home in earlier childhood. However, school teachers seemed unable to recognise that I had scant ability at all to learn instinctive ways of applying facts and to deduce hidden strategies for answering complex questions. AS makes it much harder to pick out sneaky little hidden clues and guess which two of the small details in a homework question should be put together to discover a strategy for answering it. This is terrifying. These items are not usually apparent from literal reading and literal application of the strategies already known. AS gears you to absorb facts. So when educational theory sneakily decides not to teach facts directly, but to try to teach an instinctive skill at working out ways to arrive at leaps of understanding, the effect on our stress levels and ability to cope is catastrophic.

Fairness and bearable quality of life are the morally right positive objectives. Straight away this tells you that any positive experience has to be found in escaping from and undoing any unfairness and bad deals from life, and their effects. It has to include being the character who you truly and fairly are, instead of the character who arrogant know-alls tried to force you to be, like some teachers and child psychiatrists did with me.

Only fairness is positive

This importantly identifies a wrong path, which logically will not lead to positives, but which is popularised disturbingly often. The path of passive acceptance, one-sided forgiving, now often glibly called 'letting go'.

Where the hell did the illogical idea come from, often heard in psychology, that holding onto intense passion against your oppressors and keeping your energy focused purposefully without end on the fight against them, somehow harms you? Never has a shred of factual evidence been shown to support that most perverse idea, which turns common sense upside down. So why would anyone buy it? Lack of common sense, desperation to listen to advice from a boffin – these weaknesses are easy to exploit. Any professional who claims you would be happier just accepting life as a maltreatment has left it for you, is on the maltreaters' side not on yours.[3]

Forgiveness only has virtues when applied to truly regretted effects of innocent errors, not to deliberate evil. It is a virtue of kindness to be understanding of human fallibility, willing to be tolerant and caring when a person has made a genuine error and is penitent of it in proportion to its effects. This is what the forgivist talk in religion should be applied to: a virtue of not being primitively cruel about

---

3   Editors' note: many people with AS find great solace in engaging
     in their special interests; indeed they can be a positive and hugely
     important aspect of life. However, it must also be acknowledged that
     if the focus of special interest is somehow inappropriate, or if the
     interest 'takes over', precluding important development in other
     areas of life, then it may be necessary to take steps to support the
     individual in a way that benefits him/her in the longer term, always
     taking into account the fact that a special interest may be a crucial
     part of their lives.

each other's mistakes. When remorse for deliberate wrongs is expressed it should be given a hearing on its merits, but you are looking to find that the person was somehow conned into doing something they would not naturally think was right. Then you can see that person as a fellow victim, feel compassion for them, but simply move your non-forgiveness on to the party who conned them.

This is civilised tolerance. To be a positive experience it should work by common sense fairness, not by burying the unchangeable fact that a negative happened. The naff ideas of 'let go' or 'move on' are a cruel trick whose function is to keep you docile, to let uncaring professionals park you in a corner out of sight. The rational state of a logical mind, hence of an Aspie mind, with strong moral reactions, is anger.[4] Of course anger is less cosy than complacency, and keeps painful thoughts in the front of your mind. Of course that has to be a personal choice. It makes sense to me because all painful memories are reduced in intensity by the positive self-esteem of knowing that you are doing something about them, fighting back.[5]

This obviously is not paradise, but it is far more personally satisfying.[6] The positive rewards for making this choice are how clean you feel, and the certainty that anger at injustice always makes an impact. In these feelings there is a great sense of security. You know exactly where you stand. You always know that nobody who has maltreated you has won your acceptance of it. Speaking out and campaigning on the cause of a life pain makes a difference to it and to its toll on you, and that is the best positive experience I can ever have.

---

4   Editors' note: whilst this may be the case for the author, it may not be the same for other individuals on the autism spectrum.

5   Editors' note: anger is a natural part of life but should only be used when not harmful to one's own or others' mental or physical well-being.

6   Editors' note: while this is satisfying for the author, it is not necessarily applicable to all others.

Contrast it with letting go, which leaves the pain and its toll undiminished. One gives you some empowerment over how you are perceived and treated, the other gives you none. Depressingly none indeed. There can't be any uncertainty in the choice. Emotional positivity and political rights are inseparable.

Positive is conscious of negative

I have belonged to an Aspie local group whose chair was also a parent and she had found the strategy of picking out positive experiences necessary and valuable to stand up to the voices playing down her child's life prospects in the early days of Aspie awareness. Putting her feeling into practice, she used to ask us to share a positive experience at the start of each meeting.

I had a potential problem with this, as sharing an inanely happy trivial event is not my perspective on life at all. Survivorship of serious injustice is perpetually at the front of my awareness and must never be comfortably masked out of others' minds. The sick idea of feeling good despite past wrongs and not dwelling on them I will have nothing to do with. So I put into practice a countervailing idea:

Every positive experience I ever gave to that group was either an undoing of some of the negatives in my past, or a campaigning success on an issue that came from those negatives. I showed that I will find my positives from the fightback against negatives. I showed that these are the type of positives with a real practical value, for yourself as well as for knowing you are doing good for other folks. Who can contest that helping other folks' lives to become less unjust should be the most fulfilling type of positive feeling worth achieving? It is a perfect moral proof of the rightness of persevering with pet causes, keeping your fairness issues in your foremost sight and not letting go.

With AS I would not expect to pass at the social dynamics of overseas charity work. But AS has surely helped me with perseverance and independence from peer approval, to win through for the cause that defines my life and soul: making school more libertarian. Knowing I was factually right has always been positive, from the times when I was alone with nobody's backing at all, into the time when it has been absorbed seamlessly into the autism awareness work that vindicates all my school troubles and shows they are widely shared by others.

There is a positive I am particularly thrilled to have tried out in a group setting and shown that it works. I have long attended a volunteer project to gain more gardening skills, itself a positive experience of the informal learning in free easygoing conditions that I stand for morally. In its member meeting, I actually got them to agree to ban saying 'Unfortunately, that's the way it is.' And it worked – nobody found they had any need to say it.

This was putting into practice my observations, as an Aspie outsider, of unjust social behaviours. I have often noticed that the word 'unfortunately' gets used as a weapon, by officials and mean-spirited characters, to assert refusals to play fair, and the idea of a 'way it is' to override rationally argued cases for changing ways. Both are heard often in blunt-toned macho posturing. They defend injustice, as the reformer proposing an adaptation to make something fairer gets slapped down emotionally roughly with 'Unfortunately, that's the way it is.' This seems far more worth banning than any abstract swear word. Instead of having to share it only as an untried idea that would get slapped down and called unrealistic, I have actually scored a positive experience with it really done in practice, and successfully. It can be done anywhere.

The pain question

Here is an item about which it would be obscene child cruelty for anyone ever to say 'Unfortunately that's the way it is.' The most severe wound left, for life, by the foul up that adult authority over older children's lives caused me, is that I am a wronged child author. An adult who was formerly a child author but without the proud book to show for it now like other child authors, instead with a horror story of how all spare time for writing was swamped by monstrous homework.

That compulsory education makes it possible for such cruelty to happen crosses the line of the most elementary and literal reckoning in international humanitarian law on what slavery is. It murdered a part of my life. It creates kinship with the banned writers in the worst days of the Soviet Union. Anyone who can propose a peaceful state of mind based on acceptance of this insults its scale as an emotional injury.

After Lindsay Brown[7] in 1978, who was an inspiration, in my awareness there appears to be a long gap in successful child authors who had ordinary school lives subject to homework, and who were not already famous like Lauren Harries[8] was. If there was a cruelly wronged missing generation in the 1980s and 1990s, of whom I am one, our martyrdom makes a perfect fit with the present era of suffocatingly intensive approaches to enforcing homework, with the likes of parental signatures and teachers checking daily on effort, which emerged from the 1970s backlash against hardline values in schools. Not all child authors are Aspies, but there is a correlation. It is a great positive in

---

7   Lindsay Brown published children's novels *The Treasure of Dubarry Castle* (Hale, 1978) at age 12 and *The Secret of the Silver Lockets* (Hale, 1980).

8   TV personality Lauren, formerly James, Harries had *Rags to Riches* (1991) self-published by family at age 13, when famous as a child antiquarian.

us. As the type of children to focus on factual interests and develop well-formed ideas, we are attracted to order these thoughts into writing, which can be done as a private hobby with none of the anxieties that apply to speech. We discover writing and come to make a growing habit of it.

One thing I will very importantly not do, though every so often someone with an excessively practical mind will propose quite determinedly that I should do: I won't write as a normal adult author now, the same sci-fi/ghost novel I was writing at 12 and 13 years old, and offer it up for assessing as a normal adult's book instead of as a child's. The fight for acknowledgement of wronged child authors would not be helped by the practically automatic rejection that faces all first-time fictional works by adults, and even if it were to be published, it would be obviously morally wrong to allow myself to be seen only as an adult author. It would be a marketing exploitation. Society is prone to make a routine of supposing that it is always a positive to try for any achievement. In this case, as in the case of pursuing school achievements under authoritarian conditions, the reality when reasoned through turns out to be negative. There is a life lesson there: take care to scrutinise an idea's potential negatives before you decide it would be positive. Mindless optimism is never positive.

Everything I write or say about wronged child authors is the entire meaning my existence can ever have, the positive experienced of carrying out a life mission. I have often done it on Aspie websites or forums, but my favourite incident remains my first important political milestone with it: speaking about it on record to the Scottish parliament's public cross-party group on autism in 2003. An advert here for the positive experience of the system of publicly participative parliamentary groups on particular topics, which the constitutionally innovative devolved Scotland has pioneered and which every democracy should copy.

This serious sombre approach to positivity delivers it in a really deep high-worth form. This stays with you. It is permanent, I can always reflect on it at any time of emotional need. Compare how the superficial trivial positives of 'feeling better', which are all the accepters and forgivers can get, are gone in a moment. There is no contest.[9]

Positive anger

It's positive to use my anger on behalf of others when working for autism needs through my local group and the participative Autism Network in Scotland – that is another of our innovations that every country should have.

Driven emotions and standing by my issues are the natural complement to all the other good practical successes for us; for example, getting a job in a sensible, planned way, through an autism employment service that discusses your balance of strengths and limitations rationally with the employer. This method works, where the nonsense of competitive jobsearch, of having to try to exaggerate your skills and play down your needs, never worked for me. The job made use of the incomplete ad hoc patchwork of gardening skills I have acquired by chance over time from ecological interests. That it worked well was an important practical positive and model for organising society more sensibly.

The same work support service backed me in asserting to the various layers of employment and training structures my biologically serious Aspie need to dress according to my sensory issues. I am among the number for whom this means shorts. My metabolism and heat sense towards fabrics is such that I cannot function comfortably with hot encased leg tendons.

My sensitivity to South Wales's nasally irritating climate, caused by damp air funnelling into the Bristol

---

9   Editors' note: we do not consider 'feeling better' to be trivial or superficial.

Channel, made my school uniform a deeply oppressive, counterproductive obstacle with a deleterious effect on my ability to focus, but lack of access to information on this, in those pre-internet times, meant I did not yet realise in childhood my identity of wearing shorts all the time. This suffering was gender discriminatory, and there was never any interest or understanding of that fact to be obtained from the media in all the years until equal opportunities laws had advanced far enough for boys to use them as a basis to fight for limb equality. Many are making news by doing that now, in an era when the fight should no longer even exist because autism awareness should already have ended all uniforms and dress codes for everyone all through society.

It hurts like hell to be a generation too old to take part in that fight *from within*.

The new version of our criteria for diagnosis, the *Diagnostic and Statistical Manual of Mental Disorders, 5th edition (DSM-5)*, has added sensory issues to the list. Helpful to this progress has been all the awareness raising work done by the autism specialists and the big organisations, in their many private contacts with doctors and medical training systems and with businesses seeking to work in autism. Why then has this never yet surfaced publicly on a significant scale? Why have the stories of sensory issues, our need as adult workers and the case against school uniforms, tended never to be aired in the leaflets and campaign literature of most prominent autism organisations? How many more hurt school experiences could have been avoided? Just recently, a local branch of the National Autistic Society (NAS) has achieved some local action positively to reverse that trend.

In Aberdeen, the NAS now runs a 'one-stop shop' local autism service and its local branch is on a drive to expand services and correct a serious local issue of doctor attitudes against adult diagnoses. At their local conference on 27 March 2015 publicising this campaign, this book's editor Luke described a stronger case of the same shorts sensory issue as I have, a decisive case where being forced to cover his sensitive limbs ruined a man's school outcome by the impossibility of focus and coping 'when your knees are on fire'. My personal independence from any diplomatic restraints upon the NAS in dealings with education services, and my position in sharing the sensory issue, have enabled me to follow up this outstanding item, circulating a notice of it to education authorities. Based on this case and conference I cited there to be a medical need for the immediate end of all school dress codes and for every child's right to be removed from any dress repressive peer group. One positive leads to another. How positive to be the Aspie with the caring passion to do what somebody needed to seize the hour and do?

So, after two entirely negative paragraphs, are you wondering where the positive can possibly be? It is here right in front of you, in the action of writing this and having it read. In testimony. To pass on the precedent I and Intowork obtained for me as an adult worker, I add a key contribution to the push for the autistic spectrum to win this one for everyone. In fact my adult precedent as cited here makes the continued existence of school uniforms impossible to sustain, alongside protecting every adult worker from dress rules.

The bearable quality of life from moment to moment, given by exercising my own clothing choices, is always a constant positive experience. That is common sense. So it is a perpetual personal boost to be in a winning position on the issue, even though it also fires a passionate anger in me at knowing that anyone has ever not been in it, and for all to be at liberty to share in this positive.

Day to day

My approach should not seem too puritanical, as I remain fully able to enjoy a tasty meal, a sea view, the Edinburgh Fringe festival and travel within my limits of confidence. These things are all releases from build-up of emotional pressure. My point is that it is only possible to enjoy such things when I know I am not letting them distract me into passivity, but sustaining my serious struggles.

That I still enjoy cold blackcurrant squash, a lifelong addiction, is actually a serious necessary triumph for personal autonomy. Common sense is that everyone at any time of life should enjoy the drinks that feel good for themselves. There may perhaps be an autistic sensory issue behind liking to wash all excess heat out of my throat thoroughly, and all the vivid red berry tastes. Every refreshing, uplifting squash drink is charged with anger, at all the hurtfully illogical family and peer pressures I suffered in my teenage years, to perceive fruit squashes as a juvenile taste that I needed to grow out of. Does this make it a negative experience? No, think about it: it makes it even more affirmatorily positive.

Is it ever positive to deny yourself and to sacrifice a positive from your lifestyle, to buy capricious, precarious favour from intolerant jerks that you know will not last? This holds for the clothes issue too.

My social life revolves only around thinking pursuits: politics, science, ecology and liberal forms of religion. Clearly no intellectual snobbery in this when I have no high-flying qualifications and no ability to cope with all the failable tests involved in getting them. It is simply a matter of always finding better social experience where folks are being more serious and sensible. This is the only type of company I can function in at all. As I am utterly helplessly unable to maintain a casual conversation beyond the first grunt, through not knowing what to say and which comment is certain to succeed, I just become stuck in a bubble of frustrated solitary silence as soon as a roomful of folks around me form into spontaneous chatty circles. I need a serious item to talk about, and a reasonable certainty that the other person is engaging with it, to effect any exchange of words at all.

It is still totally hit and miss – bad things can happen in thinking company too – but there is more of a fighting chance to get heard rationally about an unjust problem, or to be an influence towards fairer practices. In the worst cases where a group has gone bad your voice will still make a useful impact on some ears. In thick, laddish company there would be no chance whatever. Which one is the better experience?

It follows that the best company is logically bound to be the Aspie scene itself, on its broad scale. Not to rely on any particular group or website within it, as there have been serious rogue groups, both online and local. Here, as everywhere, it is always necessary to shop around to find the positives. The more that Aspies everywhere sustain a network of contact and friendships, the more self-sustaining can be its caring effect, for whenever a group goes bad, it can be exposed in the good groups. We will keep it positive by keeping ever vigilant for these negatives.

Model society

Local Asperger societies, I have found, sometimes belong to a broader local autism charity also covering parents' support, and sometimes are provided by prominent national organisations and form part of them. I have taken part in a long-running sustaining of a local Asperger society, which is totally self-run and not part of any bigger organisation. Because of this its voice is free of any need to fit with a wider agenda; it genuinely is the voice of its own members' range of thoughts. I was there when, drafting a letter on further education, we worked out that we should describe our whole range of thoughts and should not give a single group view on it, either voted on or consensual, because we came to it from a range of experiences.

Because we are a local voice, we have a seat in running our local autism plan, and we get visits asking to hear our needs when new services are being set up. You can see how much better this is for accountability than if they could just listen to a bigger organisation we belonged to, following its own agenda, and count that as listening to us! This way, the bigger organisations themselves also need to listen to us.

It's local society embracing all autistics who are able enough to discuss their own thoughts and who find our location convenient. We have no territorial boundaries and some quite far-flung friends. To achieve this picture there had to be a core number of us who are serious-minded about securing an autism community to continue long term and making friendship links nationally. The positive achievement of sustaining stably this model for a local group shows how it can be everywhere.

By having a regular cycle of social meets, we avoid the daunting discomfort of any one of us having to initiate a social happening out of the blue. This is key: many Aspies will turn away from the pain of trying to invite interest in a social meet at a random time, which others might not have the time to spare for. That is a scary thing to have to do. So it makes that much difference to have a consensus to sustain a pattern of regular meets, so that none of us has to initiate for them to happen, and all can dip in and out as suits us.

To have an active part in building up the serious standing and voice of ordinary Aspies to prevent the negative things from going on quietly under the surface: what could be a more positive, fulfilling use of our lives?

Chapter 22

Positives I Can Draw from Experiences as a Result of the Tragic Events on 7 July 2005 in London

Serena Shaw

Introduction by Dean Worton

Whilst the horrific events involved in Serena's chapter were certainly anything but positive and many lives were lost, the way that she handled the situation was remarkable. Even to people not in the immediate vicinity of such an event, having your journey curtailed by something so epic could still be very emotionally charging as you think about all the lives lost and permanently altered. It would be very difficult not to feel emotionally affected. Some people with Asperger's syndrome (AS) might be unable to really take in the devastating effects on whole families, but Serena proves that people with AS can have empathy and theory of mind. In such an upsetting scenario, having AS could create more trauma, though some can simply put logic before emotion, which can also be good.

Many people who think of people with AS as having limited ability could be proven wrong by just how much Serena used her inner resources to deal with this and to get back home safely. I like the idea of going to places with happy memories, which for people with AS (or even without) could be a good strategy and is in fact one I use myself in times of great stress – especially the beach when visiting the coast. Also, whilst not promoting religion, I can see how religion, spirituality or mindfulness could help some people with AS to make sense of their emotional feelings and put them into some kind of perspective when such a tragic event takes place. I know from personal experience that no matter what life throws at you, you need to find happiness anywhere you can and make the most of your existence.

Journey curtailed

In July 2005 I was doing a three-day course in London, connected to the work I had at that time in Hemel Hempstead, Hertfordshire. As I lived in Abbots Langley back then, I was commuting to Watford Metropolitan Station, a few miles away, leaving my car parked there and travelling into central London, shortly after 8.00 am.

On the third and last day of the course, which was 7 July, I was travelling as I had done for the previous two days, but the train unexpectedly came to a standstill a little north of Neasden, and after a few moments, the voice on the intercom instructed passengers that there would be a delay, and it was not certain how long for. The train started to move and then again, stopped.

A little time later, the train continued to Neasden station, and there it stopped. All passengers were instructed to leave the train, and board another, on a different platform. Then again, a little while later, all passengers were instructed to leave the train and go and wait on another platform.

And again, moments later, passengers were instructed to leave the station altogether, and at the entrance to the station it was then found that the station would be closed, and no-one could travel further from there by train...

Finding my way

Not knowing Neasden at all, I contemplated how I would continue my journey to central London.

I was directed by station staff to the bus routes, and then it became clear that the whole underground network into central London was suspended, but the reasons at that time were unclear.

It was only when I boarded a bus, in the direction of Wembley, a place which was known to me, and found a seat on the top deck, that I overheard conversations – there had been incidents happening in London, the reason for the train station closure – and then that I gathered it was best to make my way back home, and not to find a way of continuing my journey to the city!

The bus made its way to Wembley, where I found out where to catch another bus going to Harrow. I waited at Wembley bus station for a bus, which took a while, and many were having to rethink their journeys that day. The buses were packed with people, and I was fortunate to get a standing space on one!

Aim for what's familiar

Nearing Harrow, I of course recognised where I was heading – I knew Harrow well because of living in the suburbs there, decades ago, with my family, when they were there. That is why I headed in that direction, to what was familiar and well known!

Shocking and traumatic revelations

On arriving at Harrow, late morning, I found the nearest fastfood café to sit down with a much-needed cup of tea, and saw on their TV of course all the happenings in central London. It was with shock that I realised then from the news reports the full extent of what had been going on that morning, and why my own train journey was so curtailed. The accounts of bombings at several well-known tube stations and on a bus were truly shocking and caused me to feel a deep sense of desperation and on the verge of tears.

Refuge sought in a well-known location

Trying to compose myself, I sought refuge in Harrow for a while longer, rather than immediately heading for a bus back to Watford. I went to the Debenhams department store where I had memories of shopping with family, particularly my late mother, decades ago (yes, I drank loads of cups of tea that day!). It was a comforting place to be, a place to feel some sort of normality as well, amidst the buzz of shoppers, seemingly carrying on their pursuits as normal.

I went into the café on the top floor, and then walked around the store for some while. On the ground floor, my attention was caught by a TV in a coffee area there, showing the news bulletins of the day's events. One of the locations was Russell Square, very near to where both my brother and sister-in-law worked. I tried phoning their home phone, but there was no answer, so I left a message. I had no mobile number for my brother at that time, so all I could do was hope and pray that both he and my sister-in-law were okay. I tried other close relatives, too, but only managed to get through to answer phones.

I phoned the course providers on my mobile phone from Debenhams, to let them know that I wouldn't make it to the course that day, and they were very understanding. They advised me that most delegates had made it in that day to the last day of the course, which greatly surprised me, but then they explained that most people on the course had had much shorter journeys than me, and many of them were local to the city. They kindly agreed to send on to me any CD recordings of the sessions I missed.

The most obvious course of action following that would have been to phone my place of work, also, to advise them, as no doubt the news of the London events would have reached them and they would have been concerned, knowing that I was attending the course that day.

In hindsight

In my shocked state, I wasn't really thinking very clearly, and it rather slipped my mind to do so! I didn't manage to phone anyone else about my whereabouts! Looking back, a real sense of regret comes over me at not communicating more effectively, and not sharing more with others how the day was affecting me and the concerns that I had! Perhaps the lack of comfort I felt I received that I mention later on, was a result of not being able to express all the emotions and shock adequately! Long-term friends of my family who still lived in the area came to mind, and I wondered if I should contact them, or perhaps visit them on the way home? The bus route that I would take back to Watford would go in very close proximity to where they lived! But somehow, I was undecided about contacting them, and in the end, didn't, in case it wasn't a convenient time to call upon them just then.

The remaining journey back home

I later caught a bus to Watford. It was by now mid-afternoon, and it was rather a long journey home. I had even more time to contemplate the day, because the bus stopped at every bus stop en route from Harrow to Watford – which is about seven miles! On the journey I noted all the places of interest that held good memories, to counteract the effects of the day! When I arrived at Watford town centre, I disembarked and, still in a daze, I walked to west Watford, passing the church office, which was then located in the centre of town. I wondered whether I should call in and see if there was anyone to chat to there, but decided against it, in case no-one was available to talk. I made my way home, returning to Watford Metropolitan Station where I had begun my journey into London, early that morning – it seemed strange to have come back by such an entirely different and long-winded route, by another mode of transport! I collected my car, drove back to my home a few miles away. Still rather stunned!

Familiar territory

There were heroic tales of rescue mentioned on the evening news, as well as the full scale of the causes and tragic events that were outlined. But it all seemed so surreal, in fact, all very hard to take in. Because I knew the locations of the bombings well, the sheer shock of it was greater. They were places and transport networks that I had travelled on myself many times in the past, on trips to London and working very near to Senate House, I had often walked around Russell Square, sometimes travelled on buses, and also frequently travelled to Euston, which is not far from Kings Cross. The course I had been doing in London was also located very near to Oxford Street. So it was all rather familiar territory!

Reassuring news

I managed later to contact my brother, and was very reassured to find out that they were okay, and hadn't gone in to work at the usual time. They had been delayed because of family commitments, so had gone in later that day by bike; they hadn't taken the usual tube route to Russell Square, which would have been around the time of the London bombings. My brother was quite subdued but calm and

I didn't feel in speaking to him that there had been major incidents happening that morning.

As I look back it is with enormous relief to think of the circumstances, of how I believe that God protected them that day, although they may not even recognise God's hand – but when I think of the tragedy of the loss of life that day, the injured, the traumatised, it is my Christian faith that helps me to find hope in situations like these, and I am very grateful for what I believe was the Lord's hand on my close relatives – at the same time feeling much sadness for those who were not so fortunate.

That evening, a work colleague rang me to see if I was okay, and when I explained what had happened, she said that I had had quite an adventure!

Affects of Asperger's

But actually, the reason why it all hits me now is that in the pain and shock of events I had nobody to whom I could really express the enormous shock and relief and emotion that I was feeling that day! Perhaps it is partly due to the Asperger's syndrome which I have, that everyone I spoke to appeared to be rather 'matter of fact' and not really much affected by this major disruption and shocking occurrences in the capital city, which had caused such tragedy! I am filled with emotion every time I think of the events of that day when there was so much needless loss and pain caused to so many, that dreadful day in July 2005.

(NB: Although I only gained my adult diagnosis for Asperger's syndrome in 2009, four years after the events which I describe, and in 2005 I was unaware that I had any autistic traits, it is clear to me now that I was affected back then, as I am now, by this condition.)

People were quite kind when I told them of my experiences, but there was no real reaction from them in the way that I expected, even from relatives.

Probably the most reaction I received was from people at work, but even that was rather restrained! I guess my colleagues were trying to reassure me and to help me move on from the whole experience!

Summing up the positives

The positives that I can personally draw out of such shocking events, is that first, I strongly believe that God protected my brother and sister-in-law that day, as indeed He has done in other situations that have happened since that day. Second, that He helped me find a way home, safely, and the journey back had been through places that I already knew, and where I could find some refuge and comfort. It was a traumatic day, but I personally experienced God's care and protection.

The tragic events of 7 July 2005 have given me a different outlook on appreciating much more what I do have, and remembering to value and treasure what is important; also to be grateful, because not everyone was so fortunate that day.

Chapter 23

Interview with a Music Lover on Positive Aspects of His Life

Andy R.

Introduction by Dean Worton

Andy felt more comfortable being asked questions than writing in the usual free-flow format. From these questions, an interesting individual emerged. He has similarities with Michael (Chapter 5) in the way that music helps him as an Asperger's syndrome (AS) individual. I believe that music is therapeutic for all individuals, AS or not. Andy can really mask his autistic traits when performing, and to think that all 10,000 members of the audience probably have no clue that he is on the spectrum is marvellous. I've long thought that AS social communication issues stem from not knowing the right techniques to handle that situation. With music, Andy has the right techniques, but without music perhaps he has no toolkit to use. Aside from music, I absolutely admire Andy's journey from a bad accident to a marathon in just an 18-month period, and I also like his keen sense of direction, which a predominant neurotype (PNT) would be unlikely to have to the same extent.

What do you like most about having Asperger's syndrome?

I like the level of concentration it gives you and the attention to detail.

What do you think are the advantages of having AS?

In my new career Asperger's is definitely an advantage. Many musicians and techs are on the spectrum. I see undiagnosed Aspies all around me when I'm on tour. The single-minded (some would say bloody-minded) determination to make the show happen is essential in my chosen field. Also the ability to learn something in such detail (if you're passionate about the subject) is a real bonus. Learning and knowing about music tech really helps when you have to rebuild a pedalboard on stage in front of 10,000 people, as I have done.

Can you think of any aspect of your AS that possibly gives you an advantage over most other people?

The patience, concentration and attention to detail as described above.

What would you say has improved for you since you found out about having AS?

I was only diagnosed earlier this year. Although it has been a sharp learning curve, I decided to seek out the positive aspects of Asperger's and am discovering talents that have not been explored properly before. I am good with my hands. I am a musician, artist and am pretty good working with wood. I have started building custom-shaped and hand-painted guitars and basses. People are already asking me to take on commissions.

Can you think of at least one positive thing in your life, that is positive because of or despite having AS?

The most positive part of my life has always been the relationship with my wife. We have been together since our teens. Since my recent diagnosis we realised that we have been coping with my Asperger's for all that time without knowing or understanding it. Although I have had to work hard this year dealing with the negative aspects of Asperger's we are now coming out the other side with a really positive outlook for the future.

Could you describe your skills, abilities and talents?

I am a working musician and have improved immensely since embracing my AS. I am learning to paint and build guitars. I am improving all the time.

What do you like most about spending time alone?

Time to think is really important to me. If something big comes up in life, I need to think it through thoroughly without interruption. I like to walk or cycle in the countryside. This gives me the perfect environment to make decisions and think clearly. Now I have my destructive thought processes under control it has really sharpened my mind. I'm loving it!

What do your family, friends, colleagues appreciate most about you?

I asked my wife about this. Asperger's brings a lot of challenges to a relationship. However, she states that my ability we have named 'DadNav' is very handy. I have the ability to drive straight to a place, even if I have only been there once before many years ago. I never forget route details. I also have the ability to be able to bypass queues or road closures with my keen sense of direction.

What unfortunate situations does knowing that you have AS help you to avoid?

I now have a good understanding about how Asperger's affects me. I do not like parties and social gatherings (unless it's around live music oddly) and try not to have to attend them. Family gatherings are always difficult for me. However, since I explained Asperger's to my family they understand now why I keep disappearing to 'recharge' my social battery. The other thing that really helps is to always carry earplugs. I find some shops difficult on a sensory level so the earplugs help to turn it all down. They also come in handy in noisy, echoey places like cafés and restaurants. If I am travelling to a big city or on public transport I use an MP3 player to isolate myself as much as possible.

Does having AS ever result in you wanting to do some things on your own terms, and what are the advantages of this?

I always want to do things on my terms. It's how I work best. However, compromise is possible, but I need to understand it and the reasoning behind it. I can fully embrace it if this is met.

Do you feel that knowledge of your AS may have helped to reduce some of your traits?

No. The opposite actually. As you know, Aspies are very good at hiding their traits. I no longer feel the need to do this. When I am struggling to hear or zone in to a conversation in a noisy room, I am not shy about telling the person I am struggling in that environment due to my Asperger's.

Do you come into contact with other people with AS (including online) and how does this help you?

I joined a couple of Asperger's-based forums and they have been very helpful. I just participate in one forum now as the other was too busy and was overloading me with too many posts to read. As stated above I am sure a lot of people within the music industry are Aspies. It is one of the fields we gravitate towards. A wonderful thing happened not long ago. I was chatting to a lady who is a very dear friend. I was explaining what Asperger's is and how it affects me. She suddenly stopped me and told me that I could be describing her, that she shares many of the same traits and thoughts. I gave her a link to an online test and she scored high for Asperger's. Since then I have been helping her learn about it. Although it is sometimes difficult being two Aspies together, we connect on so many levels at a depth that neurotypicals (NTs) wouldn't understand.

Do you feel that the internet helps you as a person with AS?

Research! When diagnosed I had to understand Asperger's in as much detail as I could. This allowed me to self-analyse and work back through my life and apply Asperger's retrospectively to the incidents that confused me at the time and I have been carrying around as baggage for life. I have now been able to liberate myself from all these.

What techniques do you use for managing harder interactions and social situations?

By being open and totally upfront about my Asperger's. It saves a lot of pretence and misunderstanding.

How has knowing about your AS helped you in employment?

It's focused me into working in an area that I cope with and makes me happy. My future has suddenly become much clearer.

What advice would you give to other people with AS on being positive?

It is easy to view Asperger's as a disability. It certainly does have its downside when trying to live in an NT world. However it brings many positives too. I would encourage anyone with Asperger's to take time out to allow them to explore the 'gift' side of it. Find out what it is you love and are really good at.

Can you give examples of details that having AS has drawn your attention to and positive outcomes?

I've always had things in the back of my mind that I thought I might be good at, but have never had the chance to properly explore. When I was very young I was considered good at art. Unfortunately the education system crushed it out of me. I have had a lifelong interest in and love of music, but again school recorder lessons made me believe that I wasn't capable of playing an instrument. However, since my diagnosis I realise how the education system as it was when I was young worked really badly for me and my Aspie needs. I have therefore taken the time since my diagnosis to revisit these things. I have learnt that I can be a very proficient musician (I am playing live in a band), I have revisited my art and am working with my hands by building and painting custom guitars.

In your music career, what kind of positive attention do you receive?

I play in a punk/new wave covers band. It was the music that hit me between the eyes as a teenager.

I never like being the centre of attention so being a bassist is perfect for me. I can play guitar and I can sing but those roles are just too 'out front' for me. As a band we get lots of praise, and I know that I am lucky to be in such a good band. People seem genuinely surprised and happy how well we play the material. Having listened back to live recordings of the original bands we hold up very well.

To what extent does performing in front of an audience build your confidence?

I have learnt, since my diagnosis, to curb the unfortunate parts of Asperger's when I am playing.

I can't look anyone straight in the eye while I'm playing, at least not before I am 100 per cent comfortable with an audience. I use sunglasses as a bit of an Aspie shield. Then someone might be looking straight at me, but I can't tell because I can't see the white of their eyes. However, in most gigs there is a point when I feel comfortable, like I'm in a safe environment with friends. If and when that happens, I can remove my sunglasses and then really go for it.

Can you describe an example where your strong navigation skills have come in handy?

It happens on almost a daily basis. I travel a lot for work and can usually beat satnav into finding a new route if there is a road closure or similar.

Can you give any positive examples where you did something on your own terms?

Lots of physical challenges. I have the ability to carry on beyond the point where most would give up. I have always challenged and pushed myself beyond my physical limits. I have badly injured myself in the process though, because I would not give up or give in to pain.

When I was 19, I was in a bad crash. A car pulled out of a crossroads into the path of my motorbike. I had no chance of avoiding a collision and hit the front wing. I was thrown over the car and down the road, where I landed badly. I took off the top of my tibia, shattered my humerus and broke my opposite hand. They wired the tibia back together, removing the wire six months later. They told me then that I would never gain full movement in my leg; I would always walk with a limp and would need further surgery for knee problems in my thirties.

Eighteen months later I ran a half marathon...

I was also able to join the services and serve my country, which I did for many years.

I did have further surgery, but not until I was in my forties and after I had climbed many mountains and run a marathon and many other half marathons.

Chapter 24

Revelations on Planet Autism

Planet Autism

Introduction by Dean Worton

Office work is often a good area of work for people with Asperger's syndrome (AS) who are unsure what they want to do as it can provide a gentle introduction into working life and, while it's not for everyone, it is invariably easy to learn but involves several transferable skills, and there will always be a call for office staff everywhere. It can lead gradually to more specialised areas of work later on.

Planet Autism[1] is living proof that to have a positive experience in life there is no need to interact much with others, or even to spend much time around others; and with the internet, reaching out to others and helping them is possible without a face-to-face meeting ever taking place. The chapter also suggests that getting a higher-level education without having to endure the social environment of a traditional university can be done.

I was a late starter, me. As a child, I existed in a bit of an introverted, day-to-day bubble, I wasn't anywhere near ready to decide what on Earth I wanted to do when I left

---

1   Planet Autism is the online 'entity' of the author of the chapter.

school – it all seemed ridiculously grown up and my brain just wasn't there yet. I was still wondering what everything was all about when I had to see the careers officer. The careers officer wasn't helpful either: when I mumbled something about beauty therapy, he just said I'd have to go to college for that, which I didn't want to do then. My other straw-plucking option was 'being a secretary or something' based on a keyboard skills/typing course I had undertaken at school.

So, I kind of defaulted to 'office work', which ranged from secretarial and data input, to quality control and research support. It wasn't easy, because whilst I could do the work itself well enough, having to be part of a team was tough and I struggled with time-keeping in all my jobs. I didn't understand all the office politics and people confused me – they were all so cliquey, back-biting and sometimes plain mean. So I muddled through as best I could, always feeling I was in the wrong place and that there had to be something better out there.

There came a point where I discovered temping. This suited me because if I hated the place, the work or if the people were awful I could just get moved to another assignment. I became something of a 'professional temp'! This was positive, because it brought me into contact with permanent jobs too.

Once I became a parent, I realised there was no going back for me into that office world. I had a thirst for knowledge that needed quenching, I also always felt like I had a purpose, but I didn't know what it was; it was like I was in limbo waiting for the answers to materialise. Managing the many battles and tribulations of a parent of autistic children, that purpose was unknown to me then, falling into place.

So, when both my children were finally at school, I breathed a huge sigh of relief and decided it was time for *me* once more! I enrolled on a science-related distance learning course (well, who am I to buck the trend of sciencey Aspies, eh?) and passed that with flying colours. I really enjoyed it too; I was using my brain cells at last. Bearing in mind that I hadn't studied since leaving school at 16, I was extra pleased. With that under my belt, I decided to tackle something a little tougher. I enrolled on an Open University course – another science-related one of course. I decided to work towards a BSc. I passed that first course too. Unfortunately, life got in the way, with my children being autistic and the difficulties they were having in their own education, and I had to put my studies on hold. But I had found something that made learning so accessible and easy, without any of the complications of attending a physical venue – distance learning.

With distance learning, you don't have to mingle with fellow students, you don't have to chat (although if it's about a strong interest, Aspies will have plenty to say about that!) outside of tutorials, which are a focused discussion anyway, and I decided that no matter what further education I did, distance learning would be the way to go for me.

Computers and the internet are a God-send for many autistic people. You can do so much from the comfort of your own home: learning, socialising (I have met two new Aspie friends that way) and organising your life (the comparative joy of internet grocery shopping cannot be underestimated for an Aspie!). For me, I realised that research was my thing, a definite special interest, so I undertake my research pretty much completely online. I set up my own autism awareness website, which organically expanded into the dreaded Facebook and Twitter (I realised to my relief that I could 'wing it' by putting useful information out there instead of chit chatting with people. That in itself enabled me to 'meet' other people in related areas, which has in its way (albeit often campaigning) enriched my online social experience in a safe way. I also started blogging, which as well as spreading awareness, alongside my research enabled me to take a journey into myself and analyse my experiences, as well as express my strong views!

Although my BSc has been on hold, this hasn't stopped me dipping a toe in where I could, finding special offers on two autism awareness courses (oh the irony!). I recently successfully completed a certificate and a diploma in those. Distance learning makes it possible to fit in short courses, bite-sized opportunities, whilst I am dealing with the tribulations of parenting autistic children. When the time is right, I will resume my studies again. The Open University is also really good with flexibility and having a long time to complete studies, and even tailoring your degree by including a variety of courses that interest you – that's an Aspie's dream!

This has again reminded me just how possible additional learning is and how useful a computer and internet access is to someone on the autistic spectrum, who perhaps lacks the confidence or is frozen in fear at the idea of going to a brick establishment to partake in further education and socialise.

It has made me realise just how much my Asperger's brain was underused, just how much potential I have, and made me determined to do something with that as soon as my life circumstances allow. Ultimately, it also made me find my purpose in life. I have become an autism advocate, spreading awareness of autism and the rights autistic adults and children have, and campaigning behind-the-scenes, to raise awareness and help those on the spectrum be accepted as a part of society and being a voice for change. My place in this world may be small, but hey, my voice is large!

Chapter 25

Two Very Different Birth Stories

Nat Goldthorpe

Introduction by Luke Beardon

Okay, first off – the editors' disclaimer: by including this superb chapter we cannot be seen to be promoting or condoning any type of birth experience a parent wishes to engage in. Nor is this chapter in any way aimed at criticising midwives or other professionals involved in pregnancy and birth.

Having got that out of the way, on to the chapter itself. Many mothers will talk about the wonder of giving birth; Nat does so in brilliantly eloquent style, but with an absolutely fascinating angle. What is so apparent throughout is that the 'usual' way of doing things throughout pregnancy and birth is almost diametrically opposite to what Nat needed/wanted for herself. I am in the wonderful position to know Nat and was tremendously moved by her writing; I suspect those who don't know her may well be moved too.

After reading Nat's chapter, certain things become obvious; for example, is it any wonder that for some people on the spectrum a hospital environment is one of sensory overload? I can imagine that midwives use social chat in all sorts of ways, possibly to help distract a mother in labour – but, again, is it any wonder that at a time when focus is needed more than ever, for the autistic mother this could be exceedingly off-putting? Nat articulates her perspective wonderfully, and without prejudice. Her direct style of writing (along with a depth of emotion that shines through) demonstrates something that we all know about, but do not always put into practice, and that is: one size definitely does not fit all – and in Nat's case, this includes the birth experience.

Like every experience I have ever had, my experiences of giving birth to my children are inextricably entwined with my experience and identity as being an individual on the autism spectrum. My personal journey into motherhood, as a whole, is enriched by my autism and I can see how many of my autistic traits have significantly influenced my decisions and, in the case of birth, contributed to my most positive experiences.

My first birth story illustrates how certain features of my autism, mainly social and communication differences, were challenged by other people during the birth of my son. It was due to these challenges that I made some informed choices during my second pregnancy. The choices I made enabled me to retain control of my environment and to feel that I could focus all my energy on giving birth. Obviously, no-one can guarantee to enjoy their idea of a 'perfect birth' no matter how much preparation goes in, as there are many variables that are out of one's control. However, I feel that I was able to limit the distracting social aspects which, for me, can lead to sensory overload, stress and the need for my brain to work very hard at processing language, people and the environment.

Halfway through my first pregnancy I decided I wanted to give birth at home. I cannot stand hospitals and the anxiety of having to fit in to someone else's routines. My numerous previous hospital experiences left me feeling powerless and often humiliated due to being told what to do and when to do it. They had also left me exhausted from constant sensory overload as I am hypersensitive to light, smells and noise. Rather than having to deal with all of these issues in an unfamiliar environment amongst unfamiliar people, I decided that if things went to plan, I would like to give birth in my own environment, at home. By making this decision I felt a huge shift in responsibility, from the maternity service to myself and this felt very empowering. I instantly dropped my previous interests and began to devour all the information I could dig up on pregnancy and birth, becoming more and more aware of my body and baby and with an increasing sense of calm and trust in the birth process. My first pregnancy was a blissfully positive experience where, at one point, for the first time in my life, I even had a whole three weeks without anxiety. Physical changes may worry some people but I loved noticing and reading about these changes and reporting them to my partner. I was genuinely relaxed, an unfamiliar but pleasant experience. Maybe it was the relaxin hormone rushing around my body or the ultra-calm presence of my growing son. I looked forward to giving birth so much that I told a friend I hoped for a really long labour!

One thing I was surprised about was that throughout my pregnancy, my diagnosis of Asperger's syndrome was not acknowledged, despite me having declared it during my first appointment. I found that this fact, written on the first page of my notes as I had declared it, was completely ignored by every single midwife I met. This inevitably led to communication difficulties, which became more apparent as my pregnancy progressed and the scheduled midwife appointments increased. I often felt I could not express myself at antenatal appointments because I wasn't given time to process the information and to respond. This meant that I left every appointment feeling anxious, over-analysing what had been said to try and make sense of it. I became stressed because of flippant or ambiguous comments that would go over and over in my head and I found it difficult to express my wishes, for example, to say 'no' to the electronic foetal doppler and request a pinard stethoscope be used instead. However, at my appointments these anxieties were masked and I found myself smiling and nodding while inside I was screaming. I felt I was beginning to be swept along by the maternity services despite feeling strongly that I have a right to make my own choices. One thing that really bothered me was the fact I felt that all the charts and statistics were very misleading and inaccurate. I found it absurd that a tape measure over the bump is used to measure something that's curled up deep inside, and then, in the middle of talking about the weather or some such small talk, the midwife will announce, 'Baby is too small by a centimetre, you'll have to go to hospital for a scan,' or 'Baby is in the "wrong" position. You won't be able to have a home birth.' In which case I would agree at the time and then go home upset and anxious and furiously read up on all my options. In these cases I decided I wouldn't subject my baby to another scan just because the shape of my bump had changed and that I didn't see any position as 'wrong' just because it was not 'optimum'. I found the ultrasounds intrusive and when the chit-chatting sonographer prodded and manoeuvred my bump to 'get the baby moving about' I wanted to punch her in the face and walk out. None of their charts, numbers or routines reassured me, in fact they caused me anxiety. Yes, a quiet little homebirth without hustle and bustle and beeping monitors and pointless charts was definitely for me.

The home birth of my son was far from quiet, but it wasn't me making the noise, it was the midwives. They nattered about everything from the colour of my pyjamas to what they were going to eat for lunch as well as talking loudly on the phone every so often. I couldn't escape from all the people in my house and felt I was working really hard to logically process what was going on around me. I felt I had to respond appropriately, just like I do in all other social situations and this takes a lot of mental effort. My mind wasn't able to switch off and concentrate on the immense task of giving birth, and labour stopped and started every time someone new appeared. I wasn't sure of the social rules in this situation as I had never done this before. The truth is, there should be no social rules about giving birth, it's a private and primal event, but the fact there were these people in my house made it a social event. Like many autistic people, I view all people as equal. I don't see people who wear midwives' uniforms as automatic birth attendees, I see them as strangers who I have never met. To me it just felt like two random people off the street in my home. At each handover there were four midwives in my house. I had a very long labour with my son, that's a lot of handovers and a lot of strangers to meet and a lot of small talk to listen to. My home is my sanctuary, it is the only environment I feel completely comfortable in, and to have these strangers walk in and talk nonsense was more overwhelming than giving birth itself.

The birth of my son was tremendously positive in itself; he emerged looking like a little old man with all the wisdom of the universe shining out of his midnight blue eyes. But his birth was challenged by the complete sensory overload of being in the middle of a crowded and confusing, social environment. I felt hyper aware of the people around me. Although it was my own home, the strangers, their big bags of tools, the birth pool and the constant noise made it seem as though I was somewhere strange and unfamiliar. I was unsettled and anxious; anxiety is not conducive to labour. Even if I had had an experienced and silent midwife sitting in a different room throughout my labour, I feel like my environment would have been changed too much. It took me a long time to recover from the birth and all of these aspects really played on my mind. In the weeks after the birth I felt I was still trying to process what the midwives had said and I felt upset and angry. I had to find an alternative arrangement for the birth of my second child.

During pregnancy with my daughter, based on my previous experience, the one thing I feared most was the midwives and those social aspects that seemed to overshadow everything. This time I had a different midwife at each appointment and, although this might bother many people, I actually felt relieved as it meant there was no expectation to build relationships with any of them. Still, it wasn't plain sailing as the same communication issues arose. After each appointment I would analyse the conversation and try and work out what had been meant. I went away from each appointment, again feeling confused and upset and angry with their ridiculous measurements and obsession with poking and checking and monitoring. I had toyed with the idea of having an unassisted birth (birth without health professionals present) from the beginning, having heard about them during my first pregnancy. It became clear to me that this was the only way that the aspects which cause me the most anxiety (which could also then lead to complications) could be eliminated.

Therefore, no midwives were invited to the birth of my second child. My intense need for regular and absolute silence in my home was amplified during this labour just like the one before. This time though I was able to honour this and peacefully laboured alone during the silence of the night while my partner and small son slept. My contractions lasted one minute and were one minute apart right from the start, and this regularity was very pleasing to me! In the morning, clawing at the door frame mid-contraction, I woke my partner because I needed him to take over and become the decision maker and logistical thinker (as well as tea and toast maker!). We had gone over every possible scenario beforehand. I knew that I could completely trust in him to advocate for me while I withdrew into myself and switched off to the rest of the world, letting my body do one of the greatest things it was designed to do. My partner sat quietly opposite me, expecting no conversation. He passed me coconut water to sip to make sure I didn't get dehydrated as dehydration can cause irregularities with the baby's heartbeat. I squeezed his thumb through each contraction. I was barely aware of my son pottering around and looking in every so often with an unphased curiosity. For the last hour my partner called my mum over to play with my son as I needed to switch off that last part of my brain. The silence allowed me to tune in to the movements of my baby rotating and descending and I knew when to kneel down and prepare for the final moments. In true autistic style, just before my daughter was born in to my hands, I found myself meditating on four black and white scientific medical diagrams of babies rotating and descending in the birth canal, labels and all. Not exactly the waves, beaches and 'golden lights' of the hypnobirthing CD that I never got on with! My daughter broke the silence with a very loud wail, and my son, who had been watching, said matter-of-factly, 'I like that baby.' It was the best moment ever.

Both birth experiences were positive for me, and, although I know many midwives do an amazing and wonderful job, their physical presence and the social expectations from having other people around was a challenge that I felt cast a shadow and caused me too much anxiety during my first labour. I think that no woman should be expected to be engaging in social chit chat while giving birth, but maybe it is easier for non-autistic women to switch off to external stimuli and to get in to their 'zone' due to having a very effective filtering system. Having a (legal and informed) unassisted birth is not everyone's idea of a positive birth experience and I would never promote it over any other type of birth; every woman's needs, ideas and beliefs about birth are individual. For me it was an empowering, positive experience in every way.

Chapter 26

Syndromes, Spectra and Starlight

Barnabear

Introduction by Luke Beardon

This is such a beautifully written chapter, with such a vast range of qualities, it is not easy to summarise or identify any one element more worthy than another. I was hooked from the first sentence; following that, I was taken on an extraordinary journey through life as a teddy bear to computer software, to what I am guessing is astrophysics. Barnabear's ability to provide analogies between complicated scientific phenomena and the autistic brain is, simply, fabulous. With the inclusion of one of my all-time favourite words (myriad) this was a chapter that I needed to read several times; not because the level of articulation was poor (quite the opposite) but because in a mere 1952 words there were so many gems worthy of discovery. From a critique of the spectrum through to a beautifully honest appraisal of self and a bear's perspective of being an Aspie, I was left hungry for more – so, another crumpet, please...

Hi, I'm Barnabear, a teddy bear with Asperger's syndrome, at least that how it feels on the inside of who I am.

Welcome to my chapter, please come in and make yourself at home. Tea, coffee or squash? Cake, biscuits or crumpets?

I'm 4 years old tomorrow, the anniversary of my diagnosis.

I've always been a bit eccentric, popular but a loner at school, trading on my intelligence. I ended up with straight As (Bs in English) and a degree in mathematics from Cambridge.

I have a quirky sense of humour, a sidewise view of life and a family of teddy bears.[1]

I get paid to play with the innards of computers. I used to design computer chips, but moved to software many years ago.

When I'm working on a piece of software, it feels like I *climb inside and explore it*. Often I find NT[2] software a terrible mess, so I like to tidy it up. This doesn't always earn me friends. Whereas I like to order things in the software domain, I am hopelessly untidy in the physical domain.

I find computers fascinating. Inwardly, their hardware is formed in exquisite detail and their software is mathematics in motion.

Aspie brains are a bit like that.

If I asked you to sort 100 people into some order, what criterion would you choose? You could choose name, height, weight, age, birthday...all sorts of things.[3] But I'd be pretty

---

1   The world is divided into those who love teddy bears (arctophiles) and those who don't. Each thinks the other weird.

2   Neurotypicals – those ~99 per cent of the population who don't have an autistic spectrum condition. They like to think of themselves as 'normal'. Other adjectives are available.

3   Schools struggle with this sort of problem when setting *selection criteria for admissions* if the school is oversubscribed. There are strict rules about what criteria they can and cannot use for selection.

confident that you wouldn't sort them as *low-functioning* through to *high-functioning*. So why would you do this with Aspies and Auties?[4]

It is said that autism is a *spectrum condition*. What does this mean? There are phrases like 'We're all somewhere on the spectrum' and 'He's at the lower-functioning end of the spectrum.'[5] Are these terms correct, helpful or even meaningful?

Rainbows are spectra, cathedrals of light architected by refraction in myriad small raindrops.

If you split sunlight with a glass prism you get a spectrum.[6] If you pick a point along that spectrum, then you choose a particular frequency 'colour' of monochromatic light. You can even pick points beyond the visible range, for example, infra-red, and feel the warmth.

So if you say 'We're all somewhere on the spectrum,' that says that we all have our own single unique colour according to some *characteristic scale*. If that is true, then only by taking Aspies as a group would we actually construct a full spectrum.

I think that's wrong. My thesis is that each Aspie or Autie has their own individual unique spectrum that is beautiful in its own right and says much about their life. I'll explain.

Astronomers take a look along the *whole* of the measurable spectrum of starlight, examining intensity at each wavelength. The general shape of the overall profile gives the surface temperature. This is due to 'black body radiation'. As an object gets hotter, it radiates more across

---

4   Auties – people with an autistic spectrum condition other than Asperger's syndrome.

5   It is said that for people who are high-functioning, their difficulties tend to get overlooked, whereas for people who are low-functioning, their abilities tend to get overlooked.

6   Sir Isaac Newton liked to do this. He was likely an Aspie or an Autie, like Albert Einstein and Alan Turing.

the spectrum – from 'red hot' to 'white hot'. The hottest stars are in fact a bluey-white. Our sun is a yellowy-white.

Looking in more detail, the profile is not smooth. It has localised spikes and/or gaps. There are specific frequencies that are missing, depleted or accentuated. These correspond to the *spectral lines* of chemical elements such as hydrogen that can be measured here on Earth. Hence the chemical composition of the atmosphere of any star can be determined just by examining its light.

It was spectral observation of the sun's atmosphere during a solar eclipse in 1868 that led to the discovery of a previously unknown element, *helium*, named after the Greek god of the Sun, *Helios*. Helium is rare on Earth, but plentiful in stars, so the first observation of helium was at a distance of 93 million miles.

For distant stars the characteristic spectral lines are all shifted towards the red. This *Doppler red shift* is due to the star *receding*[7] and gives an idea of the distance of the star according to *Hubble's Law*. This characterises the expansion of the universe, which in turn is the primary evidence for the *Big Bang*.[8]

Moreover, the rate of recession appears to be increasing, which is a mystery. The current theory is that this is due to *Dark Energy* but we don't know what that is.

Periodic variation of the Doppler shift for local stars suggests that the star is wobbling due to the orbit of one or more planets. Many *exoplanets* have been discovered. Some exoplanets also transit across the face of their star, giving a characteristic periodic dimming of the starlight.

So there is a tremendous amount of information to be found in the spectrum of starlight. How does this relate back to autism as a spectrum condition?

---

7   Blue shift is also possible if the star is approaching.

8   Other evidence includes the cosmic microwave background radiation (CMB).

A *syndrome*, such as Asperger's syndrome, has a set of characteristic symptoms that occur in combination to different degrees, not all of which need to be present for a diagnosis to be made. Doesn't this sound a lot like the unique chemical composition of stars?

Asperger's syndrome, is characterised by a pattern of *strengths and deficits* that is unique to each individual. That's like the spectral lines in starlight.

Strengths and deficits can be affected by *environment*. That's like stars wobbling due to the orbit of planets around them and being partially obscured by planetary transits.

So if we consider a person's range of different abilities as a spectrum, then overall they will tend to have the same general shape for each person (because we're all human), but each person's spectrum will also have gaps (specific deficits) and peaks (specific strengths). It is this pattern of specific strengths and deficits that is more pronounced in people with autistic spectrum conditions. There are more of them and they are more pronounced. This pattern of pronounced strengths and deficits is unique to each person with an autism spectrum condition but may be drawn from a palette of typical characteristics in the same way that the spectral lines are drawn from a palette of elements in the periodic table.

So people with Asperger's syndrome may be good at maths, logical, good at spotting patterns, artistic, good with words, loyal, honest and so on. They may also have difficulty with eye contact, difficulty interpreting non-verbal communication such as facial expression and body language, difficulty understanding how another person may be thinking or feeling and may have prosodic speech.

It varies from person to person; there is no single stereotype.

So when I got my diagnosis four years ago, I found it difficult to recognise it in myself. I was uniquely different from other people with Asperger's and could do things they couldn't do. Even so, my pattern of strengths and deficits taken together sufficed for an Asperger's diagnosis. I thought, maybe I have a form of Asperger's that doesn't actually affect me in any way. Asperger's describes the way I am, the way I always have been. You can't turn it on or off. So it's really hard for me to spot what is 'Asperger's' and what is 'Normal'.

If I asked you whether you would want to be someone different and unfamiliar with no hope of return, would you take that risk? If you 'cured' my Asperger's then I'd be someone else, and actually I'm comfortable in my own fur, at ease with the way I am. Should you be forced to change just because you are in the minority? Certainly not; diversity can be and should be a strength.[9] Neurodiversity is important, particularly in academia and science, technology, engineering and mathematics. The work of Alan Turing, a probable Aspie, and those around him in breaking Nazi encryption shortened the Second World War, saving millions of lives.

Diagnosis has opened all sorts of opportunities for me.

Asperger's is a different way of thinking and experiencing the world. Asperger's is a distinct culture distinct from neurotypical culture. With a diagnosis I could join that culture and be accepted and understood by my brothers and sisters in autism.

Autscape is an annual three-day conference organised by people with autism for people with autism. I feel totally accepted there as I am – I can relax and enjoy an environment where autism is in the majority.

An outreach relationship developed between myself and a local Asperger special school. I sent them books, and then taught computer engineering there on a voluntary basis.

---

9   Available at www.ted.com/talks/temple_grandin_the_world_needs_all_kinds_of_minds, accessed 27 October 2016. Temple Grandin (2010) – 'The World Needs All Kinds of Minds'.

My colleagues provided junk computers, which my group of three students would take apart and rebuild into systems, which they then could have in their rooms.

There was a bird box with a camera in it. We built a server to capture images and turn them into time lapse videos. We wrote a website to present the pictures. So we covered a lot of areas.

I do feel that there is a potential synergy between experienced engineers and Asperger special schools that goes deeper than just the occasional Science, Technology, Engineering and Mathematics (STEM) event (which in any case aren't autism-friendly). I would like to see more of these outreach relationships to develop the deep skills and potential that many autistic students have.

With a diagnosis I have been able to take part in research at the University of Southampton. This is both an opportunity to be included and to give something back.

I have taken up several speaking opportunities to relate how Asperger's forms an integral part of my life and how I experience it.

Recently I spoke at the University of Southampton at the first of their 'Digital Bubbles' seminars. I put forward the theme 'Autism – what can be invented?'.[10] The researchers have taken this theme forward, and have plans to elicit ideas for problems and inventions to solve them with a view to selecting one and realising the solution in real life.

I find myself for the first time an author, writing these very words.

Like many Aspies, I don't want a cure. Generally Aspies want to be accepted for who they are, to be included and to

---

10 'Innovative technologies for autism – critical reflections on digital bubbles' is a seminar series funded by the UK's Economic and Social Research Council (ESRC). Available at http://digitalbubbles.org.uk, accessed 27 October 2016.

be supported to attain their potential to live their lives to the full.[11]

Asperger's is who I am, my self-identity, my culture, my friendships, my talent and the reason for my success. Yes, there may be downsides but I wouldn't choose to be different from the way I am.

Now, how about another cup of tea?

---

11   There are many good autism organisations, such as Autism Hampshire, who do an excellent job of supporting and including people with autism, their families and those who love them. I salute each and every one of these fantastic organisations.

Chapter 27

Turning a Negative into a Positive

Alex Wilkinson

Introduction by Dean Worton

This is a great chapter. I share Alex's gratefulness for diagnosis in later life. It might not work for everyone, but where people do have a capacity to manage alone I believe it to be really useful because as in Alex's case it allows the Asperger's syndrome (AS) individual to gain a feeling for what works well and what doesn't work quite as well. In short, there is more chance of taking risks if the AS is not known about early on, despite some setbacks nevertheless being likely.

I like the idea of the quality check being carried out by Alex's local authority and I hope some good comes out of the recommendations that were made. I have actually not heard of an 'Aspie Trainer' before, but it sounds like a sublime idea that Alex has every reason to be proud of being a part of, and one that should be rolled out over time across the country and ideally Europe and beyond.

Defining a problem

When I first saw the brief for this book, I was confused; I mistook what Dean and Luke were looking for. I was under the impression that they wanted examples of positive experiences that have resulted from being diagnosed with Asperger's syndrome, which initially opened an existential conundrum: am I a person with autism, or am I an autistic? It's a question of DNA vs RNA – a chicken or egg quandary – which I feel unqualified to answer. The word 'with' has ten different definitions (depending on the context of its use), and, as someone who often struggles to comprehend what I read, this only highlights my difficulties, which is hardly an auspicious start! That said, I actually managed to ascertain the meaning by recognising that:

- the book is about positive experiences of living with Asperger's syndrome

- I have a diagnosis of Asperger's syndrome, and

- I've had some positive experiences, therefore

- I could write something for the book!

Consequently, I managed to allay my soporific mind-set long enough to understand what it is I should be writing, at least. Put simply, I managed to turn a negative into a positive.

So what is 'positive', anyway?

My name's Alex and I'm not a big fan of labels. I believe that if it were possible to categorise everything, then I wouldn't require an AS diagnosis since life would be less ambiguous and hence easier to understand, i.e. boring. Consequently, in my opinion positivity is all about perception; it doesn't exist in and of itself, but in relation to something else. For instance, a negative experience can lead to a positive outcome, and I hope to espouse this point with some examples.

Getting diagnosed in my late twenties

These days the general consensus appears to support the idea that early intervention leads to better outcomes, especially where autism is concerned. This might be true for some people, but I believe that I'm in a better place – despite ongoing dysthymia and anxiety – because I received a diagnosis at the age of 27. I've never felt comfortable in my skin, but always assumed it was just a phase and that I'd grow out of it. I didn't realise that I had a heightened sensory profile; I was just trying to fit in. I'm by no means loquacious, except when I feel indignant, so for the most part my conversational communication skills were sufficient.

In my mid-to-late teens I was tired most of the time, but then I was very active: school, music lessons, football, rugby, basketball, hockey, athletics and part-time work as a sports retail assistant kept me very busy; but for me, busyness is a positive. I got on okay with most of my peers; I was just a little different. I was labelled as angry by my mother and there were a few unsavoury incidents among my contemporaries (both domestically and at school), which in retrospect was probably due to sensory overload, but on the whole life could have been much worse.

It wasn't until after university, when the structure of my life broke down, that I started to notice my difficulties. Up until that point I always felt that things would get better if I continued to work hard, but then I grew increasingly depressed at my lack of progress. I struggled to find work, and then couldn't keep hold of jobs when I got them. In the end Mum managed to coerce me into going to therapy, and it was only once I'd been going to cognitive behavioural therapy (CBT) sessions for three months that she thought to mention to me that she believed I had Asperger's.

Fast-forward 12 months (which was ten months too late for Mum, unfortunately), and I finally received a diagnosis. It was an overcast, wet and windy day, and I was extremely anxious (not for the first time); it felt as if my whole life was converging upon the opinion of a clinician, so I was really conscientious when trying to get my points across. Fortunately I was proven right (I was convinced that I had AS), which was reassuring. Getting that diagnosis three years ago has enabled me to put my life into some form of context; to place a locus as some sort of starting point from which to view the world. It has facilitated a deeper understanding about myself, which has made me appreciate my accomplishments in spite of my difficulties.

I've met several Aspies who were diagnosed whilst still at school. They have received more external support than me, which has conversely made them more reliant, less self-sufficient and, for the most part, less qualified. I recognise that the autism spectrum is diverse and that everyone (neurotypicals (NTs) included) develops at different rates, so it may not be wise for me to compare myself to them. However, it's because of their situation in relation to mine that I'm grateful for a later diagnosis, because it allowed me to fail, learn and to be judged as a person[1] in my own right, rather than the proprietor of a label (or labels, in my case). It's also forced me to think about what other people are doing and thinking, which has led to better social skills. Most importantly, it hasn't changed the way my friends treat me, which I appreciate more than I could ever tell them.

Conducting a quality check

Shortly after I was diagnosed, I got involved with West Sussex County Council's (WSCC) Autism Planning Group (APG). Following the publication of the Autism Act 2009, this conglomeration was set up and chaired by the County Council to establish an Autism Strategy for Adults living with Autism in the county. The APG comprises: adult autistic self-advocates; carers of adults with autism spectrum conditions;

---

1   Admittedly, I may have been given some leeway on account of being diabetic.

NHS staff; social workers; and staff members of third-sector organisations.

As part of this, Impact Advocacy Services were commissioned to conduct a quality check on the mental health services provided to adults with autism in West Sussex. Its purpose was to ascertain the views of autistic users, carers of autistic users and mental health professionals, before making recommendations on how these services could be reviewed. Given my recent experiences of CBT, I felt able to contribute.[2] At the time I was still coming to terms with my diagnosis and I was unemployed, so I thought it would be good to do something constructive with my life.

The quality check consisted of interviews with carers of autistic adults, autistic adults themselves and a mix of secondary (i.e. councillors and therapists) and tertiary (i.e. acute/inpatient) mental health practitioners. In total the quality check team interviewed: 5 autistic adults, 5 autistic carers and 17 mental health professionals, from which we were able to compile a reduced number of case studies. These numbers may appear to be small, but when you consider that only five of us conducted the interviews (including two autistic interviewers with varying travel difficulties, myself included), combined with the size of the county (1991 km², approximately 1237 miles), and difficulty accessing mental health staff (who were very busy), it was actually quite an achievement. In addition to this we published an online survey in order to accumulate more data, before writing up a (huge) report[3] and presenting our findings to the APG. In total we came up with ten recommendations, which are still being implemented as I type (or so I've been told).

For me personally, the quality check became a bit of an obsession – I got fixated on it to the point where I wanted to work on it ceaselessly – which is hardly a surprise, given that

---

2   Let's just say that they were frustrating, so I shan't include them in this chapter!

3   It was 90 pages long, including a necessary executive summary.

I'm autistic. The whole process took just over nine months to complete, so I suppose you could call it my baby! It enabled me to demonstrate some of the skills that I had acquired through university, namely, report-writing (I wrote a lot of the report myself), data-wrangling, and PowerPoint skills, but it also allowed me to push myself to develop executive functioning skills, for instance organising the interviews, working with new people and compiling agendas for team meetings. Further, it meant I had to socialise, which is something I'd grown reluctant to do in light of the death of Mum, as well as the effort it entails. Once it was completed I felt pretty exhausted – I'd accrued stress-induced acid reflux mid-way through it[4] – but nonetheless I was happy to have to done it.

Finding meaningful employment

An upshot of the quality check was that most of the clinicians wanted training from autistic adults themselves. This led Lesley, who's my boss and has done a lot to learn about autism as a member of the APG, to suggest that we put in a bid for a small grant so that we could train some Aspies to become Aspie Trainers. The bid, submitted to WSCC, was successful and I was appointed as an Aspie Trainer/Team Co-ordinator in April 2014.

At this point we've exceeded the aims of our funding bid; in our first year we set out to deliver 12 training sessions, and ended up delivering 19 – reaching out to approximately 180 NTs in the process. Within the next three years we are aiming to become a Social Enterprise, but at the moment we're still learning our craft. We've yet to gain access to clinicians, but then (in one way or another) that's true for most people, and we're hoping to establish links within our local assessment and treatment teams in the near future!

---

4   Which has since passed.

In addition to my role as an Aspie Trainer, I'm also a Peer Trainer for Sussex Recovery College. I actually got involved via Aspie Trainers and a contact made at the APG. This lady, Wendy, has been a massive advocate for the college, and when she retires from her post as the OT Clinical Lead for Coastal West Sussex (I think that's her title) she will be sorely missed!

The college[5] empowers mental health users of all walks of life to take ownership of their mental health recovery via teaching and learning. This is done by providing courses that are co-designed and co-delivered by clinicians and peer trainers – usually one of each. At the moment I'm co-delivering two courses: Autism and Mental Health,[6] and Learning to Speak Up for Yourself. Feedback for both courses has been positive, thus far, and I hope to roll out the Autism and Mental Health course for staff at the Recovery College in due course.

I've been employed by the college for just over a year now, and whilst I find it stressful, I enjoy the thought of helping other people (although I'm not sure that I do). I've found it perversely reassuring to know that the other peer trainers have struggled, too, and that their experiences, though different from mine, have made us stronger.

Making sense of the seemingly meaningless

For me, verbosity is like the prospect of receiving an enema from a doberman: it's absurd, inefficient and incredibly messy. I often wonder if people (NTs and Aspies alike) actually know what they want to say before they start to speak. It baffles me when people complain about not

---

5   More info can be found here: www.sussexrecoverycollege.org.uk

6   With Bettina Stott, co-author of Tickle, A. and Stott, B. (2010) *Exploring Bullying with Adults with Autism and Asperger Syndrome: A Photocopiable Workbook.* London: Jessica Kingsley Publishers.

having enough hours in the day (for one, they don't own time at all) and yet they have time to talk about it (or do they?). It seems to be a simple case of opportunity cost: time spent conversing = time that could have been spent doing something else, i.e. decreasing one's workload. Of course it could be that they're keeping up appearances; it could be that they're trying to hide something; it could just be that they're venting their frustrations; or it could be that, once again, I've missed the point.

Given my proclivity towards the literal, I struggle to reconcile the message I want to convey, and the words I have at my disposal, which for the most part are an ineffable stream of consonants and vowels. When talking to someone[7] I try not to make too many inferences, in order to avoid having more simultaneous conversations than is strictly necessary, including: the one they think they're having with me; the one I think I'm having with them; the one that they think I'm having with them; the one where I actually have a clue what's going on; and the one that's actually happening... I think you get the point (or not – I don't know).

In order to overcome this, I try to remind people that I'm autistic and struggle to process language, consequently I ask them to be as concise as possible. It's easy to ask someone to explain themselves, yet it's easier to become confused when someone goes into too much unnecessary detail – less is more.

At this point you may be wondering whether what I just wrote counts as a positive experience. For me it's a question of hermeneutics – the branch of knowledge that deals with interpretation. You see, most NTs I've encountered who profess to have a good knowledge of autism aren't actually good at putting theory into practice. They might have read the words of Asperger, Attwood, Baron-Cohen, Frith, Happé, Kanner, Rimland *et al.*, but they struggle to see the

---

7   That's one other person – it becomes worse when there are more than two people having a conversation.

reality of those words (possibly because they aren't detail-orientated like us Aspies). For instance, they've read that we have difficulty understanding the thoughts and feelings of others, yet still take things personally when we point out inconsistencies and inaccuracies; they fail to realise that we're just trying to make sense of what they're saying, not ridiculing them for their inadequacies! Consequently, if those people take on what it is that I'm (not) saying, and actually use it when communicating with us Aspies, then it may (not) result in future positive experiences – for everyone. At present, it's a subjunctive positive experience, in that it could resonate with someone, just as it could send them to sleep (which is not necessarily a bad thing).

Finally, if you really want to make a positive difference, please stop projecting your thoughts onto mine. My thought processes are not yours, and I wouldn't presume to know what you're thinking. In short, I'm just different, and you're going to have to learn to deal with it – I am.

Chapter 28

Dream Big

There Can Be Another End to the Rainbow

Lynette Marshall

Introduction by Dean Worton

If I gave every contributor to this book a musical instrument as a free gift (wouldn't that be nice?), I guarantee that someone would discover a talent they never knew they had. Maybe an Asperger's syndrome (AS) band would be formed! Perseverance is key. Just think how quiet the roads would be (except for bikes) if every time someone failed their driving test, they gave up right there and asked the examiner to drop them off at the nearest bike shop. So, it's worth several attempts. Alternatively, try something else. For example, you could find out that you'll never get the hang of unicycling but then you might try something else and become a magician.

Whilst Lynette's story is not about unusual talents, she proves what can be achieved by focusing on your dreams and never giving up. Also, there's no shame in seeking support – use whatever people and resources are available. You might sometimes feel a bit cheeky asking, but in fact most people are happy to help because that actually makes them feel positive too.

I dedicate this chapter to my mum and dad, Nerys and Mike, who have always supported me.

I was nearly at the end of writing this chapter when it dawned on me that people with Asperger's syndrome like me often have to be taught or learn new skills and social rules. It is with this in mind that I considered that some people may not know the difference between a positive and negative experience as they may never have been told the difference; they may misunderstand the difference or they may just be living everyday life naturally having experiences but not thinking in any detail about them. The last may generally be best because it could be unproductive to spend too much time thinking about the past. However, I am going to try and explain what I see as a positive experience or a negative experience in case it helps anybody.

First, these experiences could relate to home life, family or friends, work life, studying at school, college or university, dealing with public services and experiences with acquaintances or strangers. Positive experiences don't have to be big like learning to drive a car or renting a house; they could be smaller like going food shopping or being kind to somebody. Each type of experience is very valid. Also, my definition of positive and negative is in my own view, in my own words and has not been lifted from a dictionary. To me, a positive experience is when a person has achieved something, is praised for something, feels that they belong in a team or a group, feels respected and treated as equal. You may feel appreciated or proud. To me, a negative experience is when you feel misunderstood (though at times the other person may not mean to be negative but may not understand AS), you feel that nasty words or actions have been aimed at you, you may feel bullied or may generally feel that you are not supported enough to carry out your job duties or to know what is expected of you. As an extra note, if you are an employer reading this I hope to highlight how a difference in attitude can help us to change what could be a potentially negative experience into a positive experience. Just having a support network or designated person and reasonable adjustments in place can make an experience more positive.

People who know me know that I am determined to succeed in almost anything that I put my mind to. For this chapter I have chosen to write about my teaching career and how I never gave up on my dream. My dream was always to be a teacher. Along the way I have fought off opinions that I would not be able to achieve this. I would challenge people with 'Why, because I have AS?' People are quick to judge but often they did not know how to reply to my directness. Plus these opinions just gave me more fire in my belly to succeed. I thought 'I will show them', and at the end of my newly qualified teacher (NQT) year as a primary school teacher for students with autism, I certainly have shown them! Not only that, but my students have made an awful lot of progress, I thoroughly enjoy my job and I am well respected for my professionalism.

I had to persevere with my career along the way for several reasons. I was not diagnosed with AS until I was 25, which meant that I had no support for it through my own schooling years. I really started to excel academically once I had my diagnosis and a reason for my setbacks. However, I always disclosed my AS on application forms as I am a very honest person. Though I cannot prove it, I believe that this put me in a less favourable position than some candidates. When I was called for an interview I had another hurdle to cross as I get very anxious during interviews. Potentially I can misunderstand, take things literally and appear unknowledgeable or unconfident by taking a long time to answer a question. The latter occurs because I can take longer to process information than the average person and I think that for me this processing time increases in times of stress or pressure. For any employers reading this, this is what a person with AS may be able to offer you: a dedicated attitude, commitment to do their best, a good sense of what is right and wrong and punctuality are seen in many people with AS.

I always try to give extra in my job for the benefit of the families. I build up positive relationships with my families, which benefit us both. My daily work includes planning, delivering and evaluating lessons, having meetings with parents/carers and other professionals, assessing work and progress, writing and evaluating individual education plans, individual support plans and one-page profiles, ordering resources, dealing with petty cash and taking my students on trips. These daily activities highlight the range of my skills and capabilities. My teaching is rated at good/outstanding, which is evidence of what I am capable of. I look forward to a long and prosperous career in teaching and I would urge anybody to aim for their dreams and don't give up. AS is experienced differently from one person to another as we are all individuals, and a different level of support or reasonable adjustments may be required. But positive experiences can be had.

I think that it is perfectly acceptable to ask for support along the way and take the support that is offered to you or at least discover the support that is available and have knowledge of it in case it is needed in the future. Once you have a diagnosis and have disclosed it (and remember that you do not have to disclose this information to everybody, just those on a need-to-know basis and these people have a duty to uphold confidentiality), there will be some opportunities to gain extra support or facilities that may help you. I have heard many people with AS or who support people with AS saying that once they become an adult the services available reduce dramatically; whilst I think that sadly this is mostly true, I also think that we can be proactive in finding the support that is available. I am lucky in that I have the confidence to do this, but generally if you are studying on a course or in a place of employment there should be somebody who will assist you.

Once I had disclosed my AS at the point of diagnosis, which was at the start of my studying for a Master's in autism, it opened up an avenue of support available to me. Though I have never qualified for Disability Living Allowance (DLA) I had immediate support from knowledgeable staff who understood me. They understood that at some point I may require extra tutorials, for essay titles to be explained to me (not so that I was told how to complete an assignment but so that I knew what the question was asking). The staff knew that I may prefer email support rather than meeting in person and extensions may have been available if they were needed. I did not need to request any extensions as it happens because I enjoyed my studies so much and work well to deadlines, but the service on offer was good. I knew that I was not to panic if I ran into difficulties during the course as I could just explain my difficulties to the staff. When I then continued to do a Postgraduate Certificate in Education (PGCE) I was offered a mentor who was willing to meet me every week, a learning contract that stated the support that I might need within the year and was shared confidentially with all staff who taught me, and a laptop on loan. A member of the IT team showed me how to use the different programs on the laptop and was at hand throughout the year if I had any issues with the laptop. I was aware that similar support was available for people with other disabilities/difficulties (e.g. those with dyslexia). I am highlighting this support to tell others what may be available and to highlight what contributed to me having a positive experience at university.

Personally I have always believed that people make their own luck to quite a high degree. I realise that this could be harder for those with AS, who may at times feel withdrawn, lack confidence or prefer to be alone. But I do think that most of these people do have their own interests – sometimes very strong interests – and that from these interests ideas may grow for a future career or a way to utilise time and earn money. I found it useful just to have one person whom I trusted who was intelligent enough to reasonably guide me through my ideas and together we formed some realistic aims for my career path.

I really do believe that all people with AS can achieve things – they are just a variety of things but this is the same in society generally. The world would be boring and not very productive if we all had the same skills and the same job! Even in every one of the young children in my class I can list skills that they have (please note that I would never do so publicly) and the subjects in which they may excel in future. I believe that given understanding staff, the right support and resources, teaching methods that are tailored to the students' needs but yet still meet targets, and a positive and suitable environment, every child can have positive experiences and therefore grow to be adults with a good level of self-esteem who have some understanding that they have a right to positive experiences like myself.

Whilst on the topic of experiences, I think that a lot of my negative experiences have derived from me feeling and thinking that I was different to others. As time has gone on I feel that I have gathered more wisdom and had more experiences that have challenged my beliefs. First, it is a fact that everybody is different anyway, and second, when I spend more time with or around people I realise that they sometimes feel or behave in a similar way to me and to my knowledge they do not have a diagnosis of AS. How factually true it is I do not know, but I have heard many people say that everybody has some autistic traits. Now I am more sociable and go out more often I definitely do not feel so alone in my quirks or ways.

One recent outing comes to mind, which I wish to share with you. I went to a pub for a meal with a group of friends and later on the pub got very crowded. One person went to stand outside for a while as they found it too busy and another commented that they struggled with too much background noise. I found this very interesting as (1) I had always thought that only people with AS and/or autism felt this way, and (2) though I have experienced both of these feelings in the past, on this occasion neither the crowd of people nor the noise was bothering me at all. It was quite enlightening to just sit there and realise this. It is experiences like this that help me to feel more positive in general as I am just a person like anybody else and actually there are similarities between us.

I am looking forward to having more positive experiences in the future in different areas of my life. I certainly want to progress in my teaching career and take on more responsibilities if possible. Another certainty is that I am sure to be found praising my students in a variety of ways appropriate to them for achieving something academically or with life skills so that they know when they have done something positive or behaved positively. As previously mentioned, I believe that everybody with AS can have positive experiences, especially if there were to be a greater awareness and/or understanding of AS in society. I hope that this chapter has been of some help and I wish you very many positive experiences in your lives.